HUMAN,
FROM
ANOTHER
OUTLOOK

Mohammad Ali Taheri

This revised edition includes all the content of the first edition in addition to the editorial changes made by native editors to enhance its readability and clarity for global readers. Furthermore, two reviewers meticulously checked all chapters of the book word for word to make sure the content, concepts, and ideas taught by Grand Master Mohammad Ali Taheri were presented identical to the Persian manuscript. We hope enthusiasts of Halqeh Mysticism find this book informative and easy to grasp.

The translation of the Quran verses used in this book were mainly obtained from the following reference: Abdullah Yousuf Ali, Al-Alfain Library Printing Publication & Distribution.
Selected translations of the poems of Hafez taken from Dr. Behrouz Homayounfar

Published in the United States by Interuniversal Press.

First published in 2007, Iran.

ISBN-10: 1939507006
ISBN-13: 978-1939507006

Interuniversal Press

This book is dedicated to Dr. Vida Pirzadeh, and all the free-thinking men and women who through the past decades have been the devout and pious supporters of a qualitative perspective on man and are my source of encouragement in every respect.

I also dedicate this book to Afsaneh Khodadoust, Mohammad Amini, Andrew Knowles, Zahra Abdi, Sara Hemmati, Sara Saie, Akram Amrollahi, Ashraf Amrollahi, Rojia Afshar, Fariba Sharifi, and Roya Pirzadeh who made the translation of this book possible through their sincere devotion and hard work, which will play a substantial role in introducing the spiritual heritage of this land to the world.

Mohammad Ali Taheri

Contents

Preface

The human being is not a creature that is left on his own, all alone in the under-world. Considering that the plan of creation has been initiated based on a calculated design and program, and that it is impossible to assume God taking action without a plan and program, or taking pointless and futile actions; therefore the creation and progress of the human being has also been initiated and travelling through its path following a grand plan and purpose. Moreover, this progress is by far more than [assumptions such as] a grudge between God and the Devil, but it is pursuing a higher objective.

The purpose is for human to reach Kamal[1] and transcendence, and for this progress to take place, certain facilities have been provisioned for the human being, which they can be discussed within the context of Divine Communal Mercy [2].

Without receiving the aid of God's Communal Mercy, human cannot go beyond a certain boundary.

One, by his own effort, can reach nowhere

Unless Your Mercy lights up his way.

-Saadi

1- The term Kamal literally means completeness and refers to the human's spiritual growth toward completion (perfection). It includes self-realization and self-awareness, meaning clarity of vision about the universe, from where and for what purpose we have come, and where we are heading to. It is attaining possessions which are transportable to the next life, and includes perceptions such as Unity and His Presence, all of which will be discussed throughout this book.

2- Divine Communal Mercy is the general Divine Grace that includes all human beings without exception and makes the path toward Kamal accessible to everyone. This Divine attribute is also referred to as Rahman.

Along this path, full of ups and downs, His mercy has always accompanied human and it always will, and it is highly improbable that man can be saved from this abyss without His blessing.

From the trap so complex and difficult

Unless the Grace of God becomes our companion, escape is impossible.

For the damned Devil earns man no gain [man cannot be saved by the Devi].

-Hafez

In this regard Hafez points out that human cannot reach the highest peak of Kamal without Divine Mercy.

That magnificent transcendental destination, we cannot dream to reach

Unless Your Blessing steps in and pushes us beyond.

-Hafez

God has thrown down His rope of mercy for human's ascension, yet, who grabs it and wants to lift himself up? Who seeks this blessing?

God's mercy has no measure or limitation, yet human does not have the capacity to exploit such abundance.

The wine of God's Mercy is boundary-less

If it seems there are bounds; it is the shortcoming of the glass encompassing the wine.

-Molana Rumi [3]

On his way, the human being is always faced with two pathways, **the path of Unity and the path of Multiplicity**. The world of Unity is applied to a world that is perceptual and enables human to perceive the universe as one Unified Body, a world where all its constituents are considered as Divine manifestations. In such a state, human finds himself in communication and unity with all parts of the universe. The world of Multiplicity is applied to a world in which human beings are separated from each other to such an extent that each individual's world is merely limited to himself; where one cannot recognize [anyone] outside the self. One is self-centered and cares only for himself, and all his attention

---

3- Molana Jalal-e-Din Mohammad Molavi, also known as Rumi.

is constantly focused on protecting his private interests and material earthly life. This trend leads to self-conflicts, and the individual's contradictions reach their maximum level. In the world of multiplicity, no two people can ever tolerate each other.

In order to benefit from Divine Communal Mercy, one must be on the path of Unity, and the facilities and necessary aids are available for those who have chosen this pathway. Those who want to follow the pathway of Multiplicity and assert themselves, must solve all their problems on their own, and expect no superior divine aid. They must rely entirely on their own knowledge, intelligence, ability, will power, and so on.

Faradarmani[4] is a subcategory of **Interuniversal Mysticism** *(Erfan*[5]*- e Halqeh*[6]*)*, and is among the Halqehes which, within the boundaries of Divine Communal Mercy, makes certain facilities available to us. The only condition necessary for this to take place is readiness to establish unity; to become united with at least one other person, so that afterwards, the third participant who is the Holy Spirit or True Sprit or … will complete the Halqeh. Upon the completion, the fourth which is God also grants and manifests His mercy via the Holy Spirit.

"Have you not seen that Allah knows whatever is in the heavens and on the earth? There is no secret talk between three people unless Allah is the fourth of them; nor between five unless Allah is the sixth; nor between fewer or more unless Allah is with them wherever they are. Then, on the day of resurrection, Allah will make them aware of the truth of their conducts. Surely, Allah has full knowledge of all things." (Quran; Mujaadalah: 7)

The connecting individual (connector), can share his heavenly portion with others, "…those who spend out from what We have provided for them" (Quran; Baqarah: 3), and move toward unity and fulfill his mission of being a **Monothe-**

4- Faradarmani is considered as a complementary and alternative medical treatment, and is one of the services provided by God's Communal Mercy. For a full description please see Chapter 2.

5- Erfan: Also spelt Irfan literally means knowing. It is used to refer to both Islamic mysticism and the attainment of spiritual knowledge springing from direct insights. Erfan overlaps greatly with Sufism. For a full description please refer to page 84 "General Definition of Erfan".

6- Halqeh: literally means circle. Every Halqeh is a hypothetical circle that has three members. Upon the formation of the Halqeh, divine grace immediately flows through it and the necessary actions will take place. Each Halqeh provides us a special facility.

ist (Movahed). Those who believe in Divine Unity, encourage human beings to unite and make peace with themselves and the Universe in order to reach that. Such people are called **Unitarians** *(Movahed)* [7].

The current book is a small token of a great movement toward **uplifting Iran's Erfan**. It serves as a reinstatement of Iran's position as a powerful base for mysticism in the world, and that it is still capable of gaining worldwide credit by unlocking and unveiling the secret insights and undisclosed awareness which are the spiritual resource [heritage] of this land. Let it also be a message to those who, due to lack of such enlightening guidance, have been attracted to the mysticism or false-mystic movements of other nations and cultures; Let us not become an example of this poem of Hafez:

For years my heart was in search of the Grail (Cup of Jamshid) [8]

Not knowing he had always had within; what he begged from strangers.

Let us sit around our own table and eat from the spiritual food that is the fruit of centuries of struggles of this land's mystics [9] and lovers of the path of truth. Let us also offer this to the world and pave the way for the new generation and save them from the lack of identity and mental void.

Wishing you Divine Awakening,

Mohammad Ali Taheri

7- In Interuniversal Mysticism this term exclusively means as it is defined above, and its definitions in Christianity and other religions and branches are not meant.

8- The Cup of Jamshid (Jam-e Jam) has been the subject of many Persian poems and stories. It was believed to be filled with an elixir of immortality and it could reveal the secrets of the universe when one looking into it. Here means divine knowledge.

9- Aref = precise word for Master in Erfan or an Erfan Master. Also sometimes called Sufi, Dervish, Pir.

Chapter One

Halqeh Mysticism

The curls (Halqehes) of alluring chain of the Beloved's hair

Keeps away the troubles.

The one who is out of this chain

Is disengaged from all these ventures.

-Saadi

Interuniversal Mysticism *(Erfan-e Halqeh)* is a mystical[10] outlook, which conforms to the framework of Iran's native Erfan. This Erfan is based on the connection or Ettesal to the several circles or Halqehes of the Interuniversal Consciousness and the entire path of exploration and transformation is by means of connection to these Halqehes.

Divine Grace flows in different forms through various Halqehes which are indeed the very Halqehes of **Divine Communal Mercy** that can be practically utilized. For the reason that Ettesal cannot be established through skill, technique and method, in this branch of Erfan there are no skills, techniques and methods involved, and there is no place for personal abilities.

10- Mysticism is the pursuit of achieving communion with (or conscious awareness of) the Ultimate truth, Divinity, or God. In mysticism this is made possible through direct experience, revelation, or intuitive insight.

The fundamentals of the Interuniversal Mysticism *(Erfan-e Halqeh)* are:

• Becoming familiarized with **Divine Communal Mercy** and **Divine Specific Mercy** and its several Halqehes, in theory and in practice.

• Becoming connected (linkage or *Ettesal*) to the **Positive Network** (Interuniversal Consciousness) and avoiding the **Negative Network**.

• Becoming an (impartial) observer (**surrendering**)

• Identifying **Min Dun-e-Allah**, [taken from the Quran's words meaning anything other than God or instead of Him] and avoiding it.

• Identifying *Kamal*-**based Mysticism versus Power-based Mysticism**, moving toward *Kamal*-based mysticism, and avoiding power-based mysticism.

• Understanding **Knowledge of** *Kamal* as the sole part of human possessions that is transferable to the next life.

• Full attention to the meaning and **insight** behind the ceremonies and rituals [pertaining to prayers and worship], instead of relying merely on their external performance and formalities.

• Attention to **eagerness and enthusiasm** [11] which is the currency of the world of Kamal. In this world, the most passionate are indeed the wealthiest of all, and in this world all there is, is the reward of eagerness.

• Full attention to human's **free will**, which determines Kamal and the quality of a human being's progress.

Interuniversal Mysticism *(Erfan-e-Halqeh)*

Erfan-e-Halqeh examines the mystical concepts both in theory and practice, and since it is inclusive of all people, everybody -regardless of their race, nationality, religion, faith, or personal beliefs- can accept its theoretical aspects, and experience and make use of its practical applications.

• **Principle:** The purpose of this mystical branch is to help

human beings reach Kamal and transcendence, a movement from the world

---

11- Enthusiasm is an inner burning desire for discovering the truth and becoming closer to the God.

of Multiplicity toward the world of Unity. In this regard, all efforts serve to bring human beings close to each other and to avoid any factor that brings about separation and disunion.

Divine Communal Mercy

Love treats rich and poor alike

This scale balances stones and jewels as equals.

-Sa'eb Tabrizi

God has bestowed a special attention upon human, and out of His Love He has treated human with total mercy. This **Communal Mercy** includes all human beings, but human has the choice to use or refuse it. There is by no means any obligation to benefit from the Communal Mercy; it is a table that is set ready everyday, yet not everybody proceeds to have a bite.

Each sunrise, a red colored alchemy

Spreads the sunshine of Your Communal Mercy across the Walls.

-Sa'eb Tabrizi

Generally, all human beings regardless of their race, nationality, gender, age, education and knowledge, individual talents and capabilities, religion and faith, sinfulness or innocence, and purity or impurity and so on, can benefit from the Divine Communal Mercy.

The flower and the thorn are one in the sight of the nimble

How dare I become disappointed from the communal blessing of the Spring?

-Sa'eb Tabrizi

The Divine Mercy and Blessing is neither exclusive to a special group nor restricted to certain individuals. Thus, groups or people can only introduce this mercy to those who have hidden themselves from this light of salvation. In other words, they pass on to others the means of becoming exposed to this mercy. Therefore, from their heavenly daily portion, similar to their earthly earnings, they donate to others, "...those who spend out from what We have provided for them" (Quran; Baqarah: 3) and from their own connection (*Ettesal*), they also establish links for others. All religions and their branches are in agreement on this matter and the outline of all the Divine words and promising messages begins and ends with mercifulness. Thus, from any door we enter, we face His mercy.

If we consider Divine Communal Mercy from another angle, we see that man may say to God:

I am your sinful servant; where is your contentment?

My heart is gloomy; where is your light and serenity?

If you give us heaven only in return for obedience,

This is not more than a trade; then where is your forgiveness and blessing?

-Abu Saeed Abul Kheir

God has prepared the answer to man's question in advance, and in addition to rewards for his actions, He has set aside another gift to show His blessing and bestowment, in this manner there is no shortfall left for man.

The Messenger angel passes on the glad tidings of blessing

The Divine Mercy holds its way to the end.

-Hafez

In this manner whoever wishes, can come under the umbrella of God's mercifulness and benefit from it. This is the rain that falls on everybody's head. It is the sun shining on everyone that never asks "Who is receiving my light? Is he sinful or chaste, aware or ignorant, pure or not pure?...". All human beings are at the same level in the eyes of God on account of their need for His Mercy.

Behold. Last night a messenger from the invisible world

Gave this delightful news while I was drunk [refers to spiritual

ecstasy]; "His blessing is communal."

-Hafez

However, if the human being does not flourish under this rain, it is because he either has not yet exposed himself to this loving light or is living in ignorance [of its existence].

The sun of love shines on everyone

However, not all stones are the same, not all transform into gems.

-Saadi

The surge of Divine Mercifulness is an effective and valuable means for salvaging and guiding those who are lost and misled, because in this way they become acquainted with the origin of such mercy (God) and a proof of His presence. When a wise person encounters His signs, in fact he has encountered the signs of Guidance. Let us not forget that Christ the Messiah (peace be upon him) placed those who had lost their ways and had a bad name in society, in priority for benefiting from God's Universal Mercy. Extortionists, prostitutes, and villains were among those who gathered around him and find the way to Guidance at his side. In fact, his chief missionary, Paul the persecutor, was transformed from being a persecutor into an apostle. All these transformations were made possible only through being exposed to the general Halqeh of God's Mercifulness via Jesus Christ (peace be upon him). Indeed, becoming exposed to God's Communal Mercy means having the opportunity of becoming familiar with God in practice and making peace with God.

Another point is that a thirsty individual, and not a quenched one, is in need of water; those who are lost or are on the wrong path are truly in need of His Guidance and Mercy. One who has already reached the light, is not in need of anybody's helping guidance.

The water of mercy falls on the face of such earth

In whose soil are the thirsty inhabitants.

-Ohadi Maraqei

Interuniversal Consciousness

Now we will discuss the Interuniversal Consciousness or the consciousness governing the universe from the theoretical point of view. For this purpose, we offer a new topic, "The Coin of Existence," by which we can prove that consciousness governs the material world.

We assume that everything in the material world is like a coin with two faces: one face **Reality of Existence** and the other face **Truth of Existence.**

The Coin of Existence:

• **Reality of Existence** (ontological reality)

Happening and occurrence of something

• **Truth of Existence** (ontological truth)

Study of the cause of occurrence (Cause)

Study of the whyness of creation (Why)

Study of the quality of occurrence

Reality of Existence

Existential reality of something indicates that it exists; it has taken place, has happened or has been occurred whether or not we know the cause and howness [and quality] of its occurrence.

Existential reality is either observable or it exerts an effect on the environment or it can be recordable and measurable, or it may display a combination of these characteristics. For example the 'being' of a piece of stone is real, and it has come to existence regardless of whether we know how it has been created or not. It is also possible that something has a reality although we may not see or feel it. For instance, we cannot see or touch Infrared light, nevertheless it has reality, and we can measure it with the aid of some equipment and even use it in practice.

Truth of Existence

The Truth of Existence examines different aspects of existential reality such as the following:

1. The cause of existence and Howness of occurrence

For example, what is the cause of the creation of stone? Or what factors have caused the universe to come into existence? (Why it has been created)

2. The plan (purpose) of existence and the hidden aspects of existential reality

Any reality must have happened following a plan and design (plan of being). By verifying those hidden aspects, one can examine the reality's plan and purpose of being. For example, why and for what purpose has the human being come into existence? What is the Whyness of creation of the universe? (What is the philosophy of its creation)

3. The quality of existence

The existential truth examines the howness and existential quality of a reality in relation to a base point and analyzes it very closely. For example, it investigates whether a given reality truly exists in the outside world or is an illusion?

For instance, the reflection (image) of an object in the mirror has no existential truth because the image is virtual (illusory) in relation to the object. However, the image has existential reality because it has come into existence through the mirror. Therefore, it is possible for an entity in the universe to have an existential reality without having an existential truth. And vice versa, an entity might not have a reality for us, but it can have existential truth, as does Infrared light that cannot be seen through our eyes and therefore is not real for us. However, because it can be detectable via special equipment, it has existential truth in respect to our eyes.

Another example is the aura surrounding each human being. As it is not visible through naked eyes, for many years it was considered not to be real and it was supposed to be a superstition. However, finally the aura became visible through Kirlian photography. Therefore, although the human aura is not visible through naked eyes, it has existential truth. Thus, existential truth studies the howness and quality of being of a subject or a phenomenon.

Now in order to understand "The Interuniversal Consciousness" we need to closely examine the existential truth and existential reality of the material world or the universe itself, so here we put forward the subject of "the illusionary or virtual world."

The Illusory or Virtual World

Let us imagine a blade that can spin around its central axis as shown in Figure 1-A. Does the blade have existential reality in the still position?

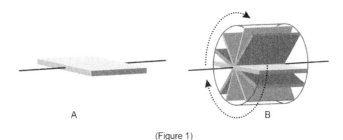

(Figure 1)

The answer is yes, because this blade has come to existence, and it is real. Now if we make the blade spin rapidly around its middle axis (as in Figure 1-B), what we see is a cylinder. The diameter of the cylinder's base is the blade's diameter and cylinder's height is the blade's thickness (Figure 2).

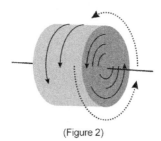

(Figure 2)

Now the question is: Is this cylinder real? Yes, it is real because it has occurred. However, another question is: Is this cylinder also true? The answer is "no" because such a cylinder has no external existence and disappears as soon as the blade stops moving. Therefore, the cylinder is a virtual volume created from the motion of the blade. Thus, although it is real, it lacks existential truth.

Following this observation and the subsequent discussion, we raise the following questions:

• Does the world around us have existential reality?

Surely the answer is "yes" because we exist and we can observe the world.

• Does the universe have also existential truth?

To answer this question, we examine, very briefly, the structure of the universe within the scope in which we have been able to observe and investigate.

As we know the world around us is made of Matter and Energy. (In essence, the universe is composed only of Energy. Please refer to Mono-form World, page 52.)

First, we consider the Material element which includes the cosmic bodies, and we study their structure. These bodies are made from molecules, and molecules consist of atoms. Atoms in turn are made of elementary particles as well as their anti-particles. This manner of succession continues to negative infinity inside the atom's core, where neither an initiation point nor any ending can be found.

As Shah Nemat-Allah Vali, the poet, says:

We have fallen to an endless world.

There is no beginning for us, or an end.

Now we study an atom as the building block for the structure of universe's creation. To examine more precisely, we envision an atom to be the size of a football field, so the atom's nucleus (in comparison to the size of the atom) would be the size of a football (Figure 3). If we observe this atom from a farther distance, it looks like a giant sphere. Now we raise further questions:

• What causes the form and the volume of this giant sphere?

This volume results from the electrons' movement, which is called the "electron cloud."

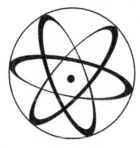

(Figure 3)

• Does this huge sphere have existential reality? Surely the answer is "yes" because the sphere has been created and is real.

• However, does it also have existential truth?

As soon as the electrons stop moving, this volume which has resulted from movement of the electrons disappears before our eyes in an instant, and only the nucleus with the size of a football remains. Therefore, we conclude that this volume does not exist in the outer world but is the result of motion and is therefore virtual.

Now, we study the nucleus of an atom in the same way. We know the nucleus of an atom consists of Protons and Neutrons. As you see in Figure 4, a proton spins around its axis. The neutron also spins very rapidly around the proton in the opposite direction. It also spins around itself. Consequently, the spin of a neutron around a proton produces a disc, a virtual volume.

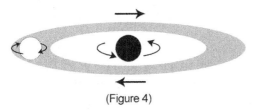

(Figure 4)

Now if protons and neutrons stop spinning, this volume also disappears, and from the whole atom, whose volume is considerably less than before, only the elementary particles remain.

In this manner, if we continue to penetrate into the particles inside the nucleus and on their different levels, stop them from moving, we will see the volumes created by these particles disappear one after the other without a trace. In summary, a collection of infinite elementary motions form the nucleus of an atom, and the atoms form molecules, and from molecules the material part of the universe has been formed. Accordingly we can say:

> **The material world is made from motion.**

We can also reach the same conclusion from another perspective. In modern physics, matter is defined as a condensed wave, and wave in turn is considered as motion. So the entire material world (be it matter or energy) has been made from waves, which are themselves caused by motion.

After this brief and simple explanation, now we can reply to the question of whether the material world has existential truth. The answer is that, while the material world has been created from motion, all its various manifestations also result from motion, and as explained before, all the manifestations of motion are virtual; therefore, the material world is virtual and lacks existential truth.

After understanding that the material world has been created from motion, we consider another question:

• Which prime factor has given direction to the infinite motions in the universe in such a manner that, in the midst of all these innumerable motions, a completely harmonized and purposeful system has been manifested?

The answer is that the only cause capable of directing the infinite existing motions so purposefully is an intelligent and conscious cause capable of determining that each motion in which exact direction and in which exact manner must take place in order to finally create such a purposeful, harmonious, and self-evidential system.

Hence, Matter and Energy or in other words the basis of the universe, is made from Intelligence, Awareness, or Consciousness.

> **The material world has been created from "consciousness, awareness or intelligence."**

All particles of the world, whisper in secret day and night:

"We see, we hear, we are aware,

With you non-intimates, we keep silent."

Until you desire a mass-like existence,

You won't be intimate with the heart of the inanimate, them you cannot hear

Break out of the lifeless mass-, step into world of vitality and soul.

Open your ears to particles of world, bubbling so lively

Now that the ear of your heart is opened, reveals to you how all particles are praising God

(They have been always praising, however you were not able to hear them)

So be aware and do not give in to the temptation of assumptions.

-Molana Rumi

Water and Wind, Fire and Earth are servants to the Lord.

They are alive (and obedient to His will), though to you and

me they appear lifeless.

-Molana Rumi

• **Principle:** All human beings can come to an agreement and reach a common viewpoint based upon the consciousness governing the universe. After testing and proving this consciousness, they can become conscious of the owner of this intelligence - God, so that this can become the common meeting point of all human beings beliefs and is in turn fortified. Therefore, the common and fundamental intellectual infrastructure among all humanity is the consciousness governing the universe, the Divine intelligence. In this doctrine, this common cause is called the "**Interuniversal Consciousness.**"

• **Principle:** The material world has been created from motion; therefore, all its different manifestations also result from motion. For the reason that any manifestation caused by motion is virtual, therefore the material world is also virtual. Since any motion requires a primary motivator to cause the movement and a directing factor to give it a direction, there is an awareness or consciousness governing the universe, which we call "**Interuniversal Consciousness.**" The universe is just a virtual reflection (image) of another truth and it has been created from awareness in essence, as it is shown in Figure 5.

In the view that the consciousness governing the universe must in turn have been created and governed by another source, we call this ultimate source "God or the Creator," the master of this consciousness.

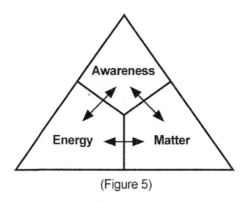

(Figure 5)

According to the above discussion, we conclude that in any given time there are three elements in the material world: **Awareness, Matter, and Energy.** For example, without Awareness, the human being cannot exploit Matter and Energy. This means that if Matter and Energy would be available to a human being, without Awareness and information he could not use Matter or Energy purposefully. Therefore, the ultimate structure of the material world is the intelligence or Awareness from which Matter and Energy are formed.

As Figure 5 illustrates, each of the above elements is convertible to the others. The conversion of Consciousness into Matter and Energy has been briefly discussed, but the conversion of Matter and Energy into Consciousness is a complex and all-inclusive discussion, which we intend to discuss separately in near future.

Figure 6 examines the particles of the material world more closely. It illustrates all the existing elements that are simultaneously present at a given time in the material world.

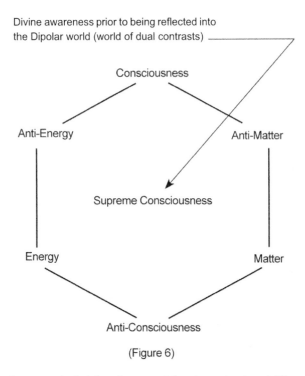

(Figure 6)

So far we have concluded that the material universe is virtual (illusory) similar to the reflection (image) in the mirror or the volume that resulted from the blade's motion in Figure 1; thus, it does not exist in the outer world.

Next, we study the universe from other perspectives:

The World's Visual Image Based on the Observer's Velocity

Let's consider an observer who is moving through space at a certain speed. As we know, when he gets closer to, or moves away from a sound or light source, the frequency and wavelength of the sound/light changes. For example, by getting closer to a sound source, the wavelength of the sound gets compressed and becomes shorter; therefore, the frequency of the sound increases. As a result, he perceives the sound at a higher pitch. In contrast, by getting farther from the source, the wavelength becomes decompressed and longer, the frequency decreases, and so he hears a lower pitched, more bass sound (Doppler Effect). The same principle applies to a light source. By getting closer to or farther from the light source, there is a frequency change, and so the color of the light and its appearance changes (Figure 7).

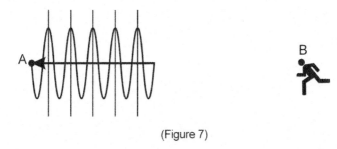

(Figure 7)

Figure 8 shows that when people get farther from the source of sound or light, the wave length increases, so the frequency decreases, and we hear the sound as more bass or see a change in the color toward longer wavelengths (red-shifted).

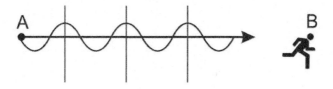

(Figure 8)

Let's think more about our hypothetical observer and what he observes before his eyes. It is obvious that as the observer speeds up, the view in front of him changes. Therefore, at a given velocity the world is perceived as a certain visual image by the observer, but the world will appear differently to him if he moves at a different velocity.

At this moment, we see the world's panorama the way it is because we are moving through space with a nearly constant velocity. This is because planet Earth is part of the solar system and revolves at a near constant velocity around its own axis and around the Sun. The solar system in turn is located at one of the arms of the Milky Way galaxy and also revolves at a certain velocity. This entire galaxy is also rotating in space with near constant velocity around another center. In this context, our perceived view of the sceneries and different color ranges is based on the ultimate velocity of our movement within space. If we lived in another galaxy, we would see different color ranges and overall different views of the world.

At significantly higher velocities, the observer perceives a considerably different view from what we see at the moment, given our position in, and velocity through space. At the moment we see our surroundings very easily, but as the velocity of our movement increases, the angle of the scenery in front of us narrows. Thus, if we could travel at the speed of light, we would in theory see a tiny hole-like opening before our eyes, nothing else!

The reason for this perception is that at the speed of light, by the time the light from the side scenery reaches the point where we are at a given moment, we have already moved past that point. Therefore, the light from objects on the sideway of our path would never get a chance to reach our eyes, and we could never observe our surroundings. The frequency of the opening which we could see would reach infinity, and it is not clear what we could observe through such a hole and how the world would look through our eyes. (Let us pause here to consider the conundrum that when the wave is condensed enough, matter will form, thus transforming the condensed wave to matter at a velocity high enough to create an impenetrable barrier in front of us [12]).

Therefore, an observer who travels at the speed of light sees the universe as just a [bright] hole with an infinite frequency. At that time, this would be the reality of his world. If such an observer has never seen the reality of our present world before, then he definitely cannot perceive or even imagine how the world looks to us - in fact he would not be able to conceive any other reality except for the universe of "bright hole."

As you can see in Figure 9, when the observer looks at his right hand side and observes the star R, star R is actually located at R' position. Therefore the observer faces two different visual fields, one is the real visual field (AB), and other is the true visual field (FE). The real visual field angle is the angle that the

---

12- "O assembly of the jinn and the men! if you are able to pass through the boundaries of the heavens and the earth, then pass through; you cannot pass through but with authority" (Quran; Ar Rahman:33)

observer actually perceives in front of him in respect to the observed object, and the true visual field angle, is the angle that the true (actual) location of the object forms relative to the observer. Now as the observer moves faster, the visual field angles AB and EF decrease such that at the speed of light, nothing is observable backwards and the compressed wave with infinite frequency appears in front of the observer.

In summary, the wavelength of energy (light) in very high velocities gets so condensed that it creates a compressed wave in front of the observer, forming a barrier (which is essentially matter). In this specific hypothetical condition which depends on the observer's velocity, the world will become very solid or dense, and regardless of which direction he intends to move, a solid wall will block his way. Therefore the universe can be considered as both finite and infinite.

As soon as the observer hits this barrier and ceases to move, the frequency in front of him will decrease and transform from the condensed form of matter into a non-condensed form of wave, and once again, as the observer speeds up, the process repeats. Consequently:

> 1.The human being's velocity through space cannot go beyond a certain limit.
>
> 2.It is impossible to travel continuously in space at velocities of very high magnitude. (Figure 9)

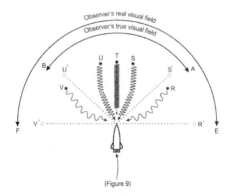

(Figure 9)

We can conclude, then, that the universe has an infinite number of appearances, and each observer sees it in a certain way depending on his velocity through space. So it is possible that other realities exist that we cannot even imagine or dream of. Does the universe possess a main distinctive appearance

then? Considering the preceding discussion:

> **The material world does not have one steady or main view. Its appearance depends on the speed of the observer, and as the observer can have countless different velocities, the material world has a potentially infinite variety of appearances for each observer.**

The World's Visual Image Based on the Observer's Eye Frequency

Each observer looks at the world with his own eyes. The eyes of each observer have a particular frequency for the number of frames per second that they can receive and interpret. In human beings, the eye frequency appears to be 24, meaning that when 24 frames pass before our eyes in a single second, we see the motion they depict as continuous (the basis of cinema). If the frequency of the frames is less than 24, the scenery before us seems interrupted and non-continuous, and by increasing the frequency of the frames, the scenery seems to move abnormally fast. Eventually at higher speeds, images would become unrecognizable. Therefore if human being sees the world in the form and appearance that we do, it is because of the frequency of his eyes, and if this frequency were a different number, the scenery of the world would appear to him differently. For example, if an object such as a ruler

rotates at the speed of 50 times (cycle) per second, what a human being sees is a circle. However if the observer's eye frequency were the same as the ruler, 50, he would perceive the movement of the ruler as steady, so he would not see the circle at all. He would see the tips of the ruler move 50 times per second.

The scenery that an eagle sees with an eye frequency of 20,000 is totally different from what a human being sees. An eagle can chase the movement of a mosquito with full concentration in every second whereas people cannot do this. This eagle would see rain as falling drop by drop, while we observe it as linear.

Another example is the snail with an eye frequency of 5; whatever a snail actually sees at such a frequency would seem bizarre to us. For example, when we are moving, the snail sees an image trail several meters long behind us (Figure 10). Only when we completely stop, does the snail see us in our actual shape. If the snail were to see a mosquito flying by, it would see a several meters long trail.

(Figure 10)

Now, if human eye frequency were infinite what would happen? Whatever an observer perceives visually is the result of the continuity of the frames. If the frequency of the observer's eyes increases, the continuity of the scenery before his eyes diminishes in a way that if the eyes had an infinite frequency, the continuity would completely disappear. In such circumstances the observer would actually see nothing because the electron movements and different frequencies would be perceived as static and still[13]. Since the electrons and the elementary atomic particles are formed from spinning and continuity, the scenery of the world would disappear from the observer's sight as his eyes' frequency increases toward infinity.

So, regarding the observer's eye frequency, the world has again countless possible visual images, and depending on the magnitude of this frequency, it can appear in potentially infinite particular ways, and so it does not possess a certain and constant appearance and is essentially virtual.

13- Previously it was discussed that motion is the essence of material world (The Virtual World; the blade example, Figure 1), therefore here failure to perceive motion at particle levels equates to observing nothing.

The Scenery of the World in View of the Observer's Perceptual Threshold

Each observer, depending on his physical perceptual threshold, sees the world in a different way. For example, what snakes can see is completely different from what human beings see because the snakes' threshold of perception is different from ours. Snakes can see Infrared light; therefore, they have very acute eyesight at night, and darkness is almost meaningless for them (night and day does not make a difference). They are also capable of seeing the temperature of objects and living creatures; therefore, what they see as the world is different from what we are familiar with and comprehend. Now let us imagine that snakes were to express their view of the world and describe what they perceive. It would definitely be very different from our view, and we would strongly disagree with each other on what we see.

A bat views the world as a confined sonographic map[14]. It can perceive only up to a limited distance, proportional to the scope of his vocal sound waves. It is obvious that the bat's visual image of the world is not comparable at all with the scenery that humans perceive. Bats' ultra-sound radar system can cover only a limited territory. If we could talk to a bat about the boundless world, he would certainly laugh at us and find it ridiculous: "How could it be possible for the world to be infinite?"

In summary, the diversity of the perceived views of the world is proportional to the number of the living creatures, from micro-organisms to the largest creatures in the entire universe. From this perspective, the world also has an indefinite number of appearances, and each observer, depending on his sensory receptors, sees it differently. This means that none of these appearances are true. Accordingly, all the physical views of the universe are virtual and none of them is true, given that if we ask which creature sees the main scenery of the world, the answer is:

14- Bats view the world based on an echolocation system. By emitting sound waves and listening to the echoes that return to them, they can form an echolocation figure in their brain, equivalent to the figure which is formed in our brain from visual stimuli.

> **The material world does not have one steady or main view. Its appearance depends on the speed of the observer, and as the observer can have countless different velocities, the mate**

A person who is born blind visualizes the world completely differently from a person who is not blind, and a person born totally deaf perceives the world differently from a normal person.

The Scenery of the Physical World in View of the Speed of Light

When we look at the night sky, we see a beautiful vista. We see so many stars that they overwhelm us with magnificence. Is this scenery before our eyes true or virtual?

The answer is what we observe at that moment is the virtual image of something that existed in this position in the past. None of the stars that we observe are actually located in the position where we see them now but they belong to the past times. This principle applies to the nearest star, the Sun, and to all other stars and galaxies that have existed for several billion years (Figure11).

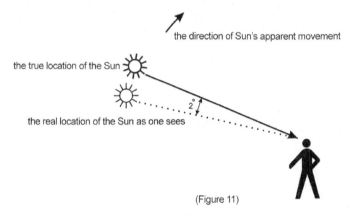

(Figure 11)

For example what we observe as the Sun at a given time is actually from eight minutes earlier. If we see an object one meter away from us, that image belongs to 0.33×10^{-8} seconds ago. In this way, all that we see is virtual perceptions, and the speed of light causes this fact; indeed, all we see is no more than an illusion.

Therefore, we cannot rely on our observations [as true], and whatever we have perceived and know as the world's image is essentially virtual.

The Scenery of the World in View of the Curvature of Space

As we know, in space a straight line is in a curved form and each moving object travels through an orbit. In other words, space is spherical and layered. Each mobile object that wants to have free movement in space must be located in one of these layers and travel along this orbit. If it intends to change the curvature's direction, it has to use energy. Now, if an observer were to look at the sky through a telescope with hypothetically infinite power, what would happen?

First, the maximum visible distance would be limited to the radius of a giant circle, and the universe would look like Figure 12 confined to this circle. Second, as he observes farther and farther, instead of seeing the front of a celestial object, he would see the side of it, up to the point where at the maximum viewable distance, instead of seeing the front of the object, he would see its back.

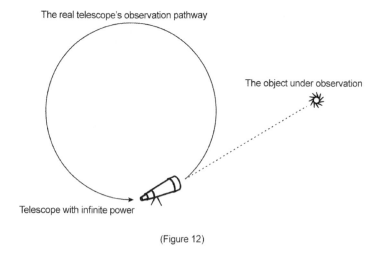

The real telescope's observation pathway

The object under observation

Telescope with infinite power

(Figure 12)

The Final Conclusion about the Virtual World

Considering all the preceding brief discussions, we conclude that from any angle at which we see the universe, it is virtual. Indeed each illusion is embedded inside an infinite number of other illusions.

Illusion within illusion is our world

Not more than a glimpse of dream inside our head.

If we do escape our way out of this delusion

Another world opens up and embraces us.

-Taheri

Why Has the Universe Been Created as an Illusionary Construct?

The illusionary quality of the material world is a sign of its God's extraordinary creativity, and although this virtual world does not have an external existence, it carries a significant truth within; as the pathway toward *Kamal* runs through this world. Human transcendence has been made possible in the midst of such an illusion; allowing him to discover and follow the pathway to *Kamal*, move toward God and reach oneness with Him (Ilayhi-Rajiun[15] : "and to Him we will return" Holy Quran.)

The concept of the illusionary quality of existence refutes the notion of God's hypothetical dependence on creation; for the reason that the universe does not possess an external existence to be assumed as an evidence of a God in need of creation.

The Mono-Form World

Principle of Structural Unity or Law of Unity in Essence

As proved in previous discussions, the material world has been created from **consciousness** or **awareness**. This consciousness has created the primary motion and has given it direction. Space and time have been created by the primary motion, giving birth to energy, which in turn has caused further temporal and spatial changes.

15- We are travelling toward Him (God) through a pathway that "returns us back to him- or the path of Ilayhi-Rajiun."

Energy is divided into two general categories, **"compressed and decompressed."** It is worth mentioning that energy itself is essentially frequency and motion, and as it has already been discussed, without the presence of intelligence and consciousness, no motion can possess direction and purpose. Therefore:

Energy is formed in the presence of the "consciousness field," and without the presence of such a field no form of energy can exist. Therefore the material world has only one dimension, and what human beings know as different dimensions (space, the third dimension and time, the fourth dimension), all make sense only within and in relation to this consciousness field; in fact, they are all created within this field.

The factor that changes the form and nature of energy is **"compression and decompression."** This factor has brought about a number of changes that have caused the world to take shape; a phase difference, based on the amount of compression, is created in each part [of the energy]. This causes succession-succession in space and in time. The phase difference originated from different degrees of energy compression, causes space curvatures and circular currents, which act like whirlwinds and can be called cosmic **whirlwinds.**

The Least and Most Compressed Energy Forms

Space spreads out more in an environment with the least compressed energy, and the sensation or perception of time diminishes in such a space, and vice versa. So space and time have an inverse relation to one another. Time is felt less at higher velocities. When some accumulated energy becomes more condensed, it loses its speed. This causes lack of equilibrium with respect to its adjacent space, and whirlwind currents occur, causing the formation of celestial bodies and galaxies. In the center of such masses, energy is more condensed.

Energy condensation has a maximum limit, beyond which it begins shifting into its anti-energy, and when energy reaches its minimum amount of condensation, this process reverses and shifts toward greater condensation, and so the cycle repeats.

Minimum energy compression ◄— Energy —► Maximum energy compression

Therefore, space and time are variable, and the universe is in a continuous repetitive cycle of contraction and expansion. Every contraction ends with a big explosion (**Big Bang**), which is also the beginning of the expansion of the next cycle. In view of this cycle, several Big Bangs have already occurred. Currently, the universe is expanding and its energies are getting less compressed. After reaching its most diluted (decompressed) state it will again contract until it reaches the most compressed state and becomes converted into its opposite (anti-energy) to create another Big Bang. In reality, the Big Bang that shaped the current universe occurred in the same manner. Upon the end of each expansion, all energies reach their most diluted level, and precisely before Big Bang occurs, all energies of the universe are converted into the compressed energy of an **"enormous black hole"**. Then, upon approaching the level of **"critical condensed energy,"** the energies suddenly shift to the direction of **"critical diluted energy."** This means that the big explosion and the ensuing expansion of the universe is a recurring phenomenon. As the boundaries of this explosion expand and in proportion to this expansion, space and time go through necessary changes. This principle shows that before the Big Bang, space had not been at its present scale but had been at its minimum quantity. Thus, the space that we now perceive had not existed in reality, and in such a condition (since time is in inverse proportion to space) time was passing at a very high speed, **"critical time."**

As the speed of the [mass of] energy decreases, it becomes more condensed and vice-versa, so that at the speed of light, compression reaches its minimum level, and consequently matter becomes equal to zero. In fact, this means that mass is equal to the degree of energy compression, so at minimum energy compression, matter is equal to zero.

The movement of any object at high speeds (one tenth of speed of light or faster) encounters a barrier that we call the **"light barrier"** (like the sound barrier). This wall is the result of wave condensation that attains a frequency equal to infinity. If this theory is true, no object can pass through this wall, and to pass through, one needs an infinite amount of energy. Because of this resistance, its mass approaches infinity. Therefore, only the decompressed form of energy can pass at the speed of light.[16]

16- "O assembly of the jinn and the men! If you are able to pass through the bounderies of the heavens and the earth, then pass through; you cannot pass through but with authority!" (Quran; Ar -Rahman: 33)

The Virtual World and the World of Science

Currently in the world of science and in modern physics (quantum physics), it is the observer who determines the structure of the universe. For example whether energy appears as wave or as particles depends on the observer.

The old perspective (the view of classic Newtonian physics) held that regardless of the observer's presence, the universe has a definite and indisputable reality, sustains its own independent form, shape, and nature, and continues to exist, so the observer's eye does not determine the scenery of the world. However, in modern physics the observer determines how and in which form a reality appears, as waves or as a composition of particles. It is not possible for the observer to see the world as both waves and particles simultaneously.

The Virtual World and the World of Erfan

Considering the above explanations, we realize that motion, consciousness, and the virtual world had already been acknowledged in the world of *Erfan*. Our mystics [Iranian masters of *Erfan*] with a high probability had grasped these concepts as reflected in various expressions in their poems. Here we briefly consider a few poems of Iranian mystics and we realize that they knew the concept of motion though they described it in their own delicate, subtle, and exquisite language.

For instance, they have likened the motion to dancing. Here, the poet portrays a beautiful image of the particle's language, with great accuracy and elegance:

We are perplexed, wandering around the mansion of Eshq (Love) and cannot figure out a way in, or a step (physical means) to climb up its roof.

Every particle (of the universe) is bursting to speak out and groan without a tongue, how can it do so?

The language of the particle is "dance."

It can't express itself, other than in an elegant dance.

-Molana Rumi

These poems demonstrate that mystics, through direct intuition had discovered that the particles of the universe have given sense and shape to the universe through the language of "dance" [motion].

All there is across the universe is love,

All together, particle to particle is embracing one another.

All the beings, hand in hand, light-winged and dancing,

Until eternity, all their vocation is playfulness and heart-ravishing.

-Unknown poet

Let's smoothly slide into dancing like a particle and conquer the Sun And arise each twilight as of the direction-, the sun of love rises up

-Molana Rumi

They had discovered this truth that an inner longing or tendency (universal consciousness) makes every particle dance and move, and an important factor in this motion is its purposefulness that directs a particle toward a specific destination.

There is a longing in each dancing particle (of the universe) Pulling it to a special destination

If you travel the world from the lowest of the low to the finest and the highest,

You don't find a particle void of this yearning.

That's the yearning, that's the one, if you know it.

From individual in a group, and from one group in a troop,

The origin of these helical threads is this yearning,

The rest is "naught" laid over "naught."

Every motion that you see springs from this desire,

From the earthly to the heavenly bodies.

For each temperament (type of character), has placed a wish (to be after for, or to desire);

This has made them move about; heading to different directions.

- Vahshi Bafghi

As mentioned before, from a scientific point of view the material world has been created from motion, but from a mystic viewpoint, it has been created from "dance," which is actually the same as motion, only in a sweet expression and more exquisite description.

Now, in order to be able to "dance," there must be a tune or music, and in order to play music, it is necessary to have a musical instrument and a musician to play it. Therefore, in mystic language further interpretations are often necessary, making the language essentially different from others.

Mystics' poetry is full of words such as dance, music, musical instrument, and musician. Some people, who are outside the world of *Erfan* and are not familiar with these kinds of expressions, view these poems with skepticism and suspicion, and in some instances consider them as profanity, accusing the world of *Erfan* of carelessness, recklessness, and inviting people to mere pleasure-seeking and indifference.

Given that one of our responsibilities is uplifting Iran's *Erfan* by unlocking its secrets and mysteries, and through precise elucidation; hereby we intend to declare the world of *Erfan* innocent and show that all those skeptical assumptions are only misunderstandings, and the words of Iran's mystics are far deeper than such superficial shallow statements. As *Hafez* says:

Excuse and forgive quarrels of seventy-two wrangling sects and arguing nations,

Unable to grasp the truth, they have followed the path of illusion.

[It was supposed to be seventy-two sects in Islam at that time]

Finally, discussing the topic of dance draws the attention to the uppermost narration that can ever be told by man; the Musician. A musician who can play such music by which all particles of the universe begin dancing, and through their dance give meaning, purpose, and sense to the universe – what a musician! Who can raise such passionate thrill with the tune of his music?

The narration of Musician is, of course, an analogy of God, who, by playing a delightful, magnificent tune, has made all the particles of the universe dance. He has created the most spectacular symphonic orchestra followed by an elegant, rhythmic, universal dance that is absolutely beyond the scope of human beings' comprehension or imagination[17].

Thus, in the world of *Erfan*, we have the following relationships:

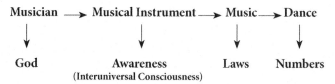

As you see, God has created Consciousness (which is equivalent to a musical instrument) and the laws governing the universe have been manifested by this Interuniversal Consciousness. In this way, God's will has been flowing and governing the universe. Accordingly, no leaf falls from a tree unless within the framework of God's authorization, which is comprised of His laws.

Laws in turn have created the numbers; in other words, the universe has been constructed from numbers. Numbers are determining the howness (manner) of the universe, and several fixed numbers (universal constants) determine the events in the universe and it is because of these numbers that we can currently live on planet Earth (These include the constant numbers of the speed of light, the Planck constant, Pi (the number π), Naperian constant, and Avogadro number. Examples of the variable numbers are the distance between the Earth and the Sun, and the acceleration of the Earth's gravity. Even a slight change in any of these numbers is a matter of life or death for human beings forever, and the same principle applies to any future changes. Yes, such accuracy in numbers and playing such a rhythmical tune are within no one's capability except God's. It is only a mystic who can hear the sound of this music that cannot be heard through the physical ears but only through insight, and can visualize this for other people through his writings. However, it is natural for someone who has not heard such a tune to deny it, regardless of how a person might logically lecture about God's abilities and immensely write about it.

17- And yet, with astrophysics and quantum physics, we are beginning to understand this symphony. Our striving to our dawning comprehension of this symphony can be considered as part of that yearning described by Vahshi Bafghi.

Although the music His lovers play, is not in tune (it is out of tune), If He plays our instruments, He brings tune to it once more

-Shah Nemat-Allah Vali

Mystics have found out that if the music that human beings produce is not rhythmic, it is their own wrong playing (doings) that have caused the musical instrument to go out of the main tune. Therefore, the mystic seeks the Musician, so that once again He tunes the musical instrument of the human being.

Come thou (the Musician) and tune my instrument

Make the Harp cry as it is bursting of tunes (has a lot to say)

Come thou! And play the Harp.

Burn and turn into the dust, this heart of mine that is cherished with love

-Amir Khosro Dehlavi

Thou (Musician), please play a simple (pure, without any rite) music

 tonight

Because tonight is the night of celebration and joyfulness of the lovers.

-Attar Neyshabouri

The Musician has played such a magical tune in the circle of Sama18

That made even the noises of chanting fade away,

to the ones in state of mystical joyfulness and rapture.

 -Hafez

He is the one who has played His most unique piece of music (through His spectacular musical instrument) as a love song and has dedicated this magnificent artwork to human beings.

The musician who plays the song of love, such a magnificent tune and instrument does He have,

Each song which He portrays, heads to a special place, a destination.

-Hafez

18- Also called Whirling Dervish, a term for a ceremony used by Sufi (branch of Erfan) practitioners which includes prayers, singing, and dancing.

Following the discussion that the universe is created from motion, and finding the word dancing as an equivalent word in the world of *Erfan*, and also considering that everything originating from motion is virtual, we now take this subject into consideration in the world of *Erfan* and we show that the mystics were fully aware that universe is virtual. By examining some of their poems, we consider this subject in more detail:

Your (physical) eyes cannot see anything but an imagination (or illusion) from the world.

Leave all these imaginations behind so that the true world could appear before your sight.

-Attar Neyshabouri

Here Attar points out that all we see before our sight is virtual and like an imagination, and the true world will appear after pulling down this curtain of imagination, which itself is another subject to be discussed, as *Rumi* says:

Without a doubt we are wandering,

Lost in the dark, the truth hidden;

Only the illusion appears to sight.

Seek that knowledge which untangles your knot (truly saves you).

Seek this before your life goes out (you die).

Give up that non-existence which looks like "alive."

Reach out for existence that appears as it has no life.

Here *Rumi* points out that virtual features have imposed themselves upon us and appeared in the form of 'being' and have taken the place of the true being. He also emphasizes that if we put aside this **virtual being**, the true being will appear. He has well understood that inside the heart of the universe, there is nothing but the Divine consciousness.

There is nothing in both worlds except God.

Don't say "No," as I know indeed you are talking about "naught."

As you open the heart of this world of hallucination,

"naught" you find inside.

Thou Ohadil, don't behold anything except God.

As if you become aware, you understand nothing is, except Him.

-Ohadi Maraghei

All other Iranian mystics have had the same opinion. For instance, *Shah Nemat-Allah Vali* in defining the meaning of the world, has called it an image and imaginary, and emphasized that only investigators of the truth would know the essential meaning of this, because ordinary people take the meaning of these sayings only as "the world is not worthy" and that it is transient and nobody should be attached to or dependent on it.

There is an image and imagination which is called 'world.'

Only the investigators of the truth understand what this talk is about.

-Shah Nemat-Allah Vali

My friend'. This imagined "world" is only a dream-,

Therefore take it (treat it) also as a dream

-Shah Nemat-Allah Vali

Sheykh Mahmoud Shabestari also clearly points that what we are dealing with is an illusion:

You are sleeping, and what you are seeing meanwhile is only a dream

And whatever you have seen from the world is of this nature (dream).

In the day of 'coming to life' or 'judgment day,' when you wake up from this dream

You will then understand all of these have been nothing but illusory.

Our mystics, all, straightforwardly state that whatever we see is merely imagination and dream. Indeed we are like somebody who is asleep. When on the Day of Judgment this curtain of illusion falls down, we will discover that whatever we used to see and consider as the truth, was nothing more than an image, imagination, and illusion; in fact, the truth has been something else. Embarrassed and ashamed are those who are captives of this virtual world and have not understood its essential nature.

Tomorrow that the presence of the truth becomes apparent,

Will be embarrassed and regretful (the travelers) whom focused on the virtual world

-Hafez

In fact we have been virtual players; or according to some mystics, we have been from the class of "The Inhabitants of the Virtual (world)," and have drowned in illusion and been deceived by the same illusion that has imposed itself upon us in place of truth.

Don't you know why I don't repent?

Because it is nothing illegitimate with me drinking wine.

To the inhabitants of the virtual world, indeed, it is (illegitimate)

And I take the responsibility for; when the true world's inhabitants drink.

-Khayyam

Drinking Wine = drinking from the wine of awareness and Divine Unity

Nobody talked to us of the secret of creation.

This truth you should not ask from the inhabitants of the illusory World.

-Parvin Etesami

Who Are Inhabitants of the Virtual World?

Inhabitants of the virtual world are those who assume that the material world is "the truth" and are deeply engaged in it and satisfied by it. They do not know for what purpose they have come to live on Earth, and what they should learn or perceive (please refer to the knowledge of *Kamal*, page 259).

The universe is like an image of His face, which has been reflected through the mirror of existence. All that we observe is considered as Divine manifestation, and wherever we look, we see only a ray of light of His face. ["Whithersoever ye turn, there is the Presence of God." – Quran; Baqarah: 115]

My Kaaba19 is by the rivers-,

19- The direction in which Muslims face during prayers is toward Kaaba and is called "Qibla." The Kaaba (or

My Kaaba is under the branches of acacia

My Kaaba is like the breeze, travels from one mountain to another, and it goes turf to turf.

My Hajar-al-Aswad20 is the glow of the flower-bed.

-Sohrab Sepehri

We have beheld the image of Beloved's face in the wineglass,

Oh thou with no clue, on our never-ending pleasure of drinking .

-Hafez

When into the mirror of the wineglass, the image of Your face was reflected,

As of the radiant wine, the mystic fell into the crude desire (of drinking)

A glance from the splendor of Your face, as emerged from the mirror

All these paintings [the universe and the creatures] fell [came into sight] through the mirror of illusions

All these images (reflected into the glass) of wine and dissimilar paintings that have appeared,

Is just one ray of light from the face of the Beloved who serves the wine (God), reflected into the glass.

-Hafez

When we are talking about the truth, it should be clear which level of truth we mean. For example, when we are standing in front of a mirror, compared to the image in the mirror, we have truth, and what exists in the mirror is virtual. But the mirror, us, and the entire universe are virtual compared to the Interuniversal Consciousness, and the *Interuniversal Consciousness* is considered as truth. Now when we compare the *Interuniversal Consciousness* with its higher level, meaning God (Creator), the *Interuniversal Consciousness* is considered as virtual and God is the absolute truth.

Qaaba) is a cuboid-shaped building in Mecca, Saudi Arabia, and is the most sacred site in Islam.

20- The ancient black stone in the eastern cornerstone of the Kaaba toward which Muslim pilgrims pray as part of their Hajj ceremony. It is revered by Muslims as an Islamic relic, which, according to Muslim tradition, dates back to the time of Adam and Eve.

From the above relationships we find that there is only one absolute truth and everything other than that is virtual. ("Everything (that exists) will perish, except God's own Face"-Quran; Qasas: 88)

The following chart shows some words that are commonly used in the world of *Erfan* and their metaphoric equivalents.

$$\frac{\text{Truth}}{\text{Illusion}} = \frac{\text{Me}}{\text{My image in the mirror}} = \frac{\text{Interuniversal Consciousness}}{\text{The universe}} = \frac{\text{God (Creator)}}{\text{Interuniversal Consciousness}}$$

Person who serves drink	Barrel Jar (Pitchen)	Cup Goblet Wine-glass mirror	Drink Liquor Wine Ruby Grape Juice
↓	↓	↓	↓
God Beloved	Intelligence Awareness Interuniversal Consciousness	Man	Awareness Revelation Rejoice

With wine color the prayer mat if the Pir [spiritual master] tells you,

For the holy traveler knows the ways and manners of the path ahead (rest houses on the way)

-Hafez

When the enlightened old wise master announced, "Thou overflow the earth with awareness! The meaning is to spread your awareness to everyone, thus:

Drink = [perceived] awareness

Prayer mat = place of prostration = earth

For example *Sohrab Sepehri* says:

My "Qibla"[21] is a red rose,

my prayer carpet is river,

I bow and put down my forehead on the light,

I perform my prayers in the temple of grassland...

The Laws of Intelligence-Awareness-Consciousness Governing the universe

• The material world has been created from consciousness, and all its constituents and particles are consciousness.

• Consciousness is neither matter nor energy, but matter and energy themselves have originated from consciousness; consequently, none of the definitions of matter and energy applies to consciousness. Therefore consciousness is neither wave (frequency) nor particle and lacks material and quantity, and no graphical diagram can be drawn to represent it. Consciousness is only a function of quality.

• Consciousness lacks time and space dimensions, its transfer and translocation do not need time [are instantaneous], and it is not a function of space.

• The whole consciousness (or collective consciousness) determines the consciousness of the constituents.

• The consciousness of each and every component of the universe affects the consciousness of all other components.

• The consciousness effect of constituents is conveyed via "emission or vibe." Consciousness emission is neither frequency nor particle in nature; it lacks chemical or physical effects, and only produces a consciousness effect.

• Consciousness of a collection of constituents, is considered as the whole or collective consciousness of the set, which predominates the consciousness of each constituent and determines the overall direction of their motion.

• A constituent's consciousness contains the whole consciousness in itself in full.

21- The direction in which Muslims face during prayers is toward Kaaba and is called "Qibla."

The Laws of Consciousness-Intelligence-Awareness Governing Human Beings and Cells

• Each cell has its own unique consciousness that includes the descrition of its duties.

• Supervision over the cellular consciousness is the responsibility of the human being's "mental body" which determines the consciousness quality and duty description of each cell.

• Communication between the cellular consciousness and Interuniversal Consciousness is through the mental body.

• Consciousness possesses emission.Constituents in the vicinity of one another are affected by each other's consciousness emission; and individuals are also affected by each other's consciousness emission.

• Human being's thoughts, feelings, and illnesses (cellular emission) also possess consciousness emission.

• The collection of individuals' consciousness emission makes up the "collective soul" of that set; thus, we have collective soul of a family, a society, or humanity.

• The cellular consciousness can be corrected directly through the Interuniversal Consciousness; and also through the consciousness of Matter.

• When the "correction of cellular consciousness" is accomplished directly through the Interuniversal Consciousness, there will be absolutely no errors and we will encounter no side effects. However, when we use the Matter's consciousness, first, there is a probability of wrong diagnosis, and second, it is possible that its con sciousness would be suitable for certain cells but not for others.

Step of Wisdom and Step of Eshq (Love)

The human being is always faced with two steps, *the step of Wisdom* and *the step of Eshq (Love)*:

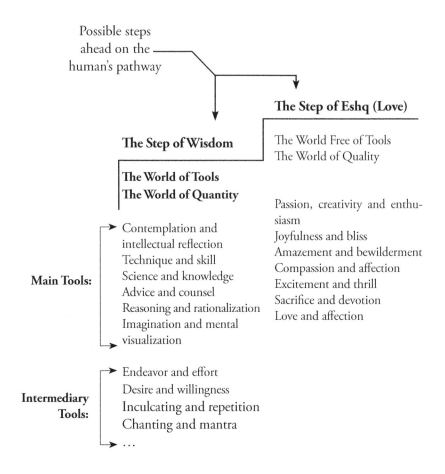

Possible steps ahead on the human's pathway

The Step of Eshq (Love)

The Step of Wisdom

The World Free of Tools
The World of Quality

The World of Tools
The World of Quantity

Main Tools:

Contemplation and intellectual reflection
Technique and skill
Science and knowledge
Advice and counsel
Reasoning and rationalization
Imagination and mental visualization

Passion, creativity and enthusiasm
Joyfulness and bliss
Amazement and bewilderment
Compassion and affection
Excitement and thrill
Sacrifice and devotion
Love and affection

Intermediary Tools:

Endeavor and effort
Desire and willingness
Inculcating and repetition
Chanting and mantra
…

All the human being's interactions with the universe are based on one of these two types of approaches. What is encountered at each step has no direct use on the other step; however, the resultant outcomes can be studied on the other step. For example, a person in love cannot be convinced through advice, reasoning, and rationalization to give up his affection for his beloved, nor be convinced to love somebody else. So, at the step of *Eshq* it has been said:

"The feet of rationalists are wooden

The wooden foot is so disobedient! "

-Molana Rumi

Also we cannot create enthusiasm in somebody through technique, science, knowledge, or intellectual contemplation and force him to show the enthusiasm and passion [enabling him] to compose a poem. In other words the world of Eshq is the world of heart and is not influenced by technique, skill, and so on, but follows its own path where no logical advice and counsel would be effective.

Where I am from, is far away from where the advice comes

Thou Saki (wine server in Farsi)! Pass it around and pour that

life-giving goblet into my heart.

-Molana Rumi

None of the consequences gained in the world of *Eshq* may be transferable or comprehensible through writing and books.

"Wash up all the papers if you are our companion and classmate

Because the lesson of love is written in no book"

-Hafez

Shah Nemat-Allah Vali has composed on the subject:

Worshiping ignorantly is nothing but temptation,

The ways of enthusiasm are not learned at school.

You never become mystic through Logic and Geometry

As the grounds of love can't be found through such spheres.

That silent spot is unutterable,

The first step is to forget all your books and learning.

- Sa'eb Tabrizi

The world of **Eshq** is not accessible through struggle, endeavor, and will power, as if, for example, someone says he would try to fall in love within the next few hours or he would endeavor to find the truth of the universe.

Never can you reach the ultimate jewel of desire by your own endeavor.

It's mere illusion to have this done without intermediary. (Divine help)

-Hafez

No one can be forced to compose a lovely poem or to be excited, nor can one pressure himself to be surprised or astonished. The affairs of the world of Eshq are spontaneous and must be created in a self-initiated unprompted manner. On the step of wisdom; we consider a lover as crazy, because affairs of *Eshq* cannot be justified through wisdom.

How can I versify these lines

Whilst the root of my good health is spoiled?

There is more than one insanity within this root

It is madness upon madness upon madness.

-Molana Rumi

Thus, the mystic himself not only confesses but also emphasizes on his insanity, because he well knows how prudent men would consider him. Therefore, before being addressed as insane, he has comforted everybody by confessing to be insane.

Frequently the affairs of *Eshq* are opposed by wisdom. For instance when a person sacrifices and devotes himself to others and has excessive generosity, his actions have no logical justification and are rejected by wisdom, so it is said:

Intellect won't risk a path, which may bring him disappointment Only Eshq jumps into the unknown heedlessly.

Though, true bravery belongs to Eshq not intellect,

Intellect seeks only what brings him advantage.

-Molana Rumi

So wisdom continually opposes any action that does not bring tangible and material benefits, and where man wants to follow the heart, it obstinately opposes. For example, when someone intends to experience metaphysical or supernatural phenomena, logic severely reacts against that and totally denies the possibility of the existence of such phenomena.

On the step of wisdom, there are two groups of tools, main and intermediary. The main ones are those which are used directly in practice such as science, knowledge, technique, and so on. The intermediary tools are at the service of the main ones but they are not measurable or testable, such as effort, endeavor, determination, imagination, and so on.

Unlike the world of wisdom, the world of Eshq is not describable or explicable, and experiences in this world cannot be communicated through words.

Although the tongue can guide us through

The sounds of Eshq are silent and true.

-Molana Rumi

In Eshq's sanctuary, one cannot mouth of talking and of hearing,

There; all parts (of the body) must be an eye and ear.

-Hafez

The world that explores the quality of human beings' existence and the universe is called the world of *Erfan* or the world of Eshq, the world of heart or the world free of tools.

Why all Mystics Complain about Wisdom

Mystics were among the wisest and the most learned people of their era, however all their recitations are full of complaints about logic and wisdom. Here is the question: Why have mystics always complained about wisdom?

For the following reasons:

1. Complaint about Wisdom's "Detail-Focused Perspective"

The story of the elephant[22] and the dispute among people about the form and shape of the elephant, demonstrates this detail-focused perspective of wisdom. In the story, the ignorant, imprudent people considered only touch [one of the five senses] as determinant of recognition and wisdom, and as the result of that error, they had a great disagreement. The wisdom that mystics blame is also such a detail-focused approach.

The trivial intellect ('detailed-focused' logic), is not the wisdom to be used

---

22- Please see page 103 for the full story.

for deduction.

For it's always in need, not accepting anything but the skills.

-Molana Rumi

In a workshop wherein is no path to reason and merit

Why does the weak contemplation make an arrogant judgment?

-Hafez

Take this crude wisdom to the wine house

May the pure liquor bring his blood to boil and bubble.

-Hafez

2. Complaint about Wisdom's "Matter-Of-Fact Perspective"

The most difficult stage for the mystic is when he wants to move from the step of wisdom to the step of Eshq, because logic and wisdom create obstacle on the way of this transition and may deny such a step, totally preventing him from progressing through this transition.

Wisdom says, all six directions you travel, confined are they and there is no way out.

Eshq says, of course there are ways, because I have traveled through more than once.

Wisdom sees a market and starts a trade.

Nonetheless Eshq has seen markets plentiful, far beyond wisdom's trade,

Wisdom says; don't enter, that melting [into the vanishing point] is nothing but thorns.

Love says; those thorns you're talking about, is yours! ('You' make the obstacles)

-Molana Rumi

Thus wisdom without which Eshq cannot exist, in some places serves as a hurdle for the mystic. This will lead to an intense opposition between his wisdom and Eshq, which finally causes him to cry out against wisdom and reject logic, desiring to get rid of it at this stage.

I got hold of wisdom's ear and told him, "Thou wisdom'.

Get out of here today, as I am freed from you.

Thou my logic! Leave me on my own

As today I have joined the league of Majnoon23."

-Molana Rumi

The mystic has well understood that he must leave logic at times when he intends to enter the step of Eshq:

I must become ignorant from this logic and grow to be insane.

I have already tried and tested the far-sighted intellect.

From now on, I intend to become round the bend.

-Molana Rumi

Definition of Rind

As we have seen, the world is like a coin with two faces:

- Reality of existence
- Truth of existence

If the human being only sees the reality face, he turns into a realistic person. Examining realities leads to the appearance of science and knowledge, expertise and skills, business and professions, and so on, and the individual is ultimately engaged in the games of realities. This is the phase humanity has currently reached.

If the human being only sees the truth face of the coin, he will see nothing but an illusion, and nothing makes sense for him anymore; so dealing with most daily activities such as doing business becomes meaningless. Eventually the person should head to the desert and mountains, become secluded and detached

---

23- 26. Leyli and Majnoon ("Leyla and The Madman") is a deep love story by the Persian poet Nezami Ganjavi. Qeys (Majnoon) falls in love with Leyli but there are obstacles parting them. Majnoon becomes obsessed with Leyli to the point that whatever he sees he sees as Leyli, for him everything is in terms of Leyli; hence he was called Majnoon (literally meaning possessed). Leyli and Majnoon resemble love stories such as Romeo & Juliet.

from normal life, and follow the way of love-sickness and insanity.

As you can see, each of these two ways, on its own, is imperfect and inadequate, and each has certain shortcomings. After these explanations, we can define "Rind." **A Rind is someone who considers and pays attention to both reality and the truth.** In *Erfan-e Halqeh*, based on the Rind creed, neither is reality sacrificed for the sake of truth, nor is the truth sacrificed for the sake of reality. In other words, a Rind is an individual who seeks the truth in the world of reality and vice versa, and can consider both reality and the truth. Accordingly, becoming a hermit, taking refuge in caves, undergoing mortification (strenuous self-discipline), exposing the body to harsh conditions, and so on, have no place in the world of a *Rind*.

General Definition of Erfan

Erfan means being present on the step of *Eshq*, reaching illumination, enlightenment, clarity of vision about existence and the universe, and such results definitely cannot be attained through the world of logic, science, and knowledge.

Those who see through the eyes of the (logical) mind,

are in a dream watching something illusory

(They can't see the truth behind the surface, can only touch the surface).

Although wisdom and intellect lightens and turns on the light-bulbs on the way,

However it can never take the place of the moonlight.

-Shah Nemat-Allah Vali

As a general view and in brief, the world of *Erfan* has the following characteristics and definitions (which will be discussed in a separate book):

1. Since the world of *Erfan* is the world of *Eshq* (Love), there is no use of technique, method and skill, advice, counsel and reasoning, endeavor and effort, and so on; thus it is a world free of tools, either main or intermediary.

2. The world of *Erfan* is a world beyond duty, because the world of *Eshq* (Love) is not about performing duties or fulfilling responsibilities; the world of love is

far beyond rational concerns and calculations.

On judgment day when the faces will become yellow and pale because of fear,

I hold all my Eshq to you on my hand to present,

And ask to be scored on account of my Eshq.

-Abu Saeed Abil Kheir

3. The world of *Erfan* is beyond remuneration and reward. The motivation of a lover is not gaining reward or remuneration. He is not pursuing his path based on such urges that belong to the world of logic.

The world of love,

Is a world beyond fire and fairy.

(Meaning that love is not about fear of hell, or greed of heaven, fairies)

-Sheikh Attar

Nothing we want from the Beloved, except for "the Beloved" (Him)

Thou ascetics! The Houris (angels) of Paradise bestowed on you to enjoy.

-Sheikh Bahai

4. The world of *Erfan* is not the world of fear and grief.

The world of the mystic is the world of *Eshq* (Love) (love of God); Therefore, fear, disappointment, and sorrow have no place in the mystic's loving heart ("Behold! Verily on the friends of God there is no fear, nor shall they grieve"

- Quran; Yunus: 62)

5. Sorrow, disappointment, hopelessness, distress or loneliness and so on - this subcategory of Satan's servants - has no place in *Erfan*, and the only sorrow for a mystic is the grief of being separated from God and falling away from one's origin.

Listen to this reed-flute telling a tale of separations,

Which complains of being separated from one's native land,

The reed-bed[24]"

–Molana Rumi

6. *Erfan* lays the ground-work for the unity of parts, and also communication between constituent and the 'whole'. As there are always things within the 'whole' of which the part is not aware, by approaching the whole, such [awareness-giving] messages can be received. For instance, one single cell is void of desire and wish, but the unity of hundred trillions of cells in this example make up the whole, which has desires and wishes, and follows certain purposes, whereas a single cell does not even know the meaning of desire.

7. *Erfan* means becoming resistant (shock- proof) to obstacles. On the path toward his Beloved, the mystic does not become interrupted or stopped by setbacks or strikes. Throughout the path of *Eshq* (Love), he has attained certain attributes that ordinary people lack, which enables him to transform the boat of his existence into an ocean-liner that can survive the dreadful waves of the ocean of life, whereas ordinary people encountering these waves might be tossed, overturned and fallen apart.

8. *Erfan* is the perception of *Kamal*.

The world of *Erfan* studies the awareness(es) that are transferable to the next life[25].

9. Since *Erfan* is the world of *Eshq* (Love), it is not a place for monopoly or exclusivity. It is a world that can encompass all human beings. It regards everyone as included in Divine Love.

10. As *Eshq* requires action and not mere spoken or written words and so on, *Erfan* is the world of action and [its outcomes] must be tangible.

11. The world of *Erfan* is a movement from the appearance to essence.

24- Taken from translation of Gupta 1997.

25- Please refer to chapter 4, 'Kamal versus Power'.

Introductory Description of Theoretical and Practical Erfan

1-Theoretical *Erfan* can be discussed and studied on the step

of logic. For the reason that theoretical *Erfan* necessitates discussion and study, description and clarification, it should be

introduced and should explain where it intends to take

the human being. Therefore, at this stage we must use some

description, reasoning, logic, and so on. All these tools belong to the world of logic. Therefore theoretical *Erfan* is based on the Step of logic and belongs to the world of tools.

2-**Practical Erfan** is placed on the step of *Eshq* (Love) where no possible tool can be used. Practical *Erfan* must certainly be applied on the step of *Eshq*; therefore, practical *Erfan* is a world free of tools and cannot be achieved or perceived through technique, skill, knowledge, and so on.

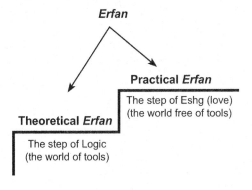

As we have discussed, the human being is always faced with two steps: the step of logic and the step of *Eshq*. The step of logic is the world of tools, skills, techniques, advice, reasoning, deductions, endeavor and effort and so on. Generally it covers a scope known as the "**World of Tools.**" The step of *Eshq* is the world of passion, enthusiasm, joyfulness and bliss, bewilderment and amazement, ecstasy and rapture, devotion, compassion, and so on. In general it is a framework that is known as the "**World Free of Tools.**" There is no ground for words, stories, books and so on in this world.

The step of logic is the basis for understanding the step of *Eshq* and all human conceptions are achieved/take place on this step. Since all the conclusions are obtained on the step of logic, **Kamal cannot be attained without the step of logic**, and therefore the step of logic and the step of *Eshq* are interdependent. According to the figure below a rational man [a person merely on the step of logic] falls in love, and a person in love becomes wise; *Eshq* is the bridge between partial intellect [Detail-focused perspective and so on] and the 'whole' wisdom. In other words, through partial intellect one cannot find the 'whole' wisdom unless being shifted from the step of logic and standing on the step of *Eshq*.

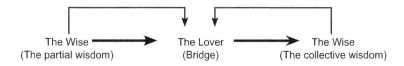

The Wise ➤	The Lover ➤	The Wise
(The partial wisdom)	(Bridge)	(The collective wisdom)

Chapter Two

Faradarmani

The souls in essence are life-giving; like Messiah's breath

Sometimes they are the wound, other times, the treat.

The souls when unveiled

Same as Messiah, each soul will speak

-Molana Rumi (Masnavi[1] first book)

On the surface; man is insignificant in the universe,

However be aware! in essence, he is the main point of the world.

A mere fly disturbs his outer shell (his physical body is frail),

Though his inner being conquers the seven skies [the treasury of all Divine knowledge].

-Molana Rumi (Masnavi fourth book)

Faradarmani is a type of complementary and alternative therapy that is totally *Erfan*-based in essence, and is considered as a subdivision of **Interuniversal Mysticism (Erfan-e Halqeh)**.This doctrine with a 30-year history is based on

---

1- "Masnavi" is Molana Rumi's greatest poetic work and means rhyming couplets.

perceptual revelations [stemming from direct insights]. It was founded by the current author, Mohammad Ali Taheri, and its foundations completely conform to Iranian *Erfan.*

In this type of therapy, the patient becomes connected or linked (*Ettesal*) to the **Interuniversal Consciousness** (the network of awareness and consciousness governing the universe - Divine Intelligence) via the Fara-therapist. Following this procedure the patient undergoes the Scanning process [in other words the *Interuniversal Consciousness* begins to assess and scan the individual]; and while the patient states some information on the process of his *Ettesal* in the form of: seeing colors, lights, feeling activity and movement of some kind of energy throughout the body, feeling heat, pain, sharp aches, pulsations, twitching or convulsions, and so on., the defective and distressed parts of the body are revealed. In this way the patient goes through the so-called Scanning process, and by eliminating the symptoms, the treatment process initiates.

Scanning means that the patient's entire existence is scrutinized by [the metaphoric magnifying lens of] the Interuniversal Consciousness, which [categorically] reveals the patient's past and current illness records. Scanning takes place in a holistic manner affecting all aspects of one's body, psyche, and *Zehn.* Sometimes during scanning, certain symptoms appear that indicate the body's susceptibility to a particular disease that could emerge and become apparent in the future. For example, the occurrence of tremors may be a sign of one's susceptibility to Parkinson's disease. Pain in the heart area or the occurrence of abnormal heartbeats without any past history of heart disease, indicates certain heart problems that will be healed and eliminated following the scanning process.

Once the patient's record of illnesses is activated, the stage of **Externalization** begins. These files could be related to any of the existential elements of the patient, such as body, psyche, *Zehn*[2], and so on. For a deep-rooted treatment to

2- Zehn, Mind or Mental body: Commonly is defined as the element or complex of elements in an individual that feels, perceives, thinks, wills, and especially reasons, in other words the conscious mental events and capabilities in an organism (Webster's Dictionary). However, the definition of Zehn in Interuniversal Mysticism is different from the above definition: In fact, the brain conveys all sensory inputs to the Zehn. Then in turn, the Zehn conveys its perceptions (about the universe, for example the decision of moving/not moving toward Kamal, being fair/unfair, and so on) to the brain. Then finally, the brain implements those decisions in the language of chemical take place, the patient must have patience and allow these Externalizations to be finished.

Important Note: The term Externalization refers to a process in which the symptoms of diseases and history of the illnesses are externalized and revealed. The history of illnesses might even go back to the embryonic or childhood stages and may include the current obvious diseases, current but undetected illnesses, hidden fears, emotional stresses and psychological obstacles, mental disorders, and so on.

In this doctrine for curing the human being, attention is directed toward all his existential constituents simultaneously, and he, as a whole, comes into contact with the Interuniversal Consciousness. Then according to the Interuniversal Consciousness's discretion, the necessary actions take place for eliminating the disorders of different constituents, and the patient progresses through the different stages of the treatment.

The name of *Faradarmani* was applied to this type of treatment because it originates from a meta-holistic view called "**Interuniversalism**" (more details on page 101).

This discipline can be effective for treating all types of illnesses, and the Fara-therapist is not permitted to assume any particular type of illness as incurable. The reason is that the treatment is performed by the *Interuniversal Consciousness* Network, and not by the Fara-therapist. Therefore, from the perspective of Interuniversal Consciousness, cure and elimination of any disorder is easily possible.

The *Interuniversal Consciousness* is the collection of consciousness, wisdom, or intelligence governing the universe, which is also called Awareness, and is one of the three existing elements of the universe. These elements are: **Matter, Energy, and Awareness.**

In the view that awareness is neither matter nor energy, the dimensions of **time and space** do not apply to it; therefore, treatment via this network is pos-

---

reactions in the body. This type of communication and interaction between the Zehn and brain will be discovered by science in future. The brain is the interpreter and the executor of the decisions of the psyche and Zehn on the body, and it is the mediator of the psyche, Zehn, and body, or a medium through which these three interact.

Note that to avoid complications, we have used the term "mental" in the text to reference the attributes of Zehn, such as "mental" confusion, by which we indeed mean confusion in Zehn.

sible from short and long distances. Also, awareness does not possess quantity, is not measurable, and as it was explained, it is only through some indicative manifestations on the patient's body that the consciousness's point of effect is revealed. Therefore, the therapist cannot attribute any of its power to himself.

Important Note: In this doctrine, contrary to many other methods (polarity therapy, for example), the actual treatment is not accomplished by the therapist, but takes place via connection (*Ettesal*) to the Interuniversal Consciousness, and the Fara-therapist merely plays the role of a [intermediary] connector to form a [symbolic] circle (*Halqeh*) called the "**Halqeh of Unity.**" The Divine Communal Mercy flows in this very intelligent *Halqeh* and causes the healing.

The essential condition for obtaining a result from *Faradarmani* is being impartially present (without any prejudice and judgment) in the *Halqeh* as an observer or a witness. Having faith or belief in *Faradarmani* is by no means necessary for becoming present or taking part in *Halqeh*.

In view of the above explanation, it is clear that treatment does not depend on the expertise or energy of the Fara-therapist, and there is no need for having any special kind of talent, power, and energy. Because the treatment is conducted by a much higher consciousness, the practitioner's personal abilities have no effect on the therapy. Consequently, the Fara-therapist does not encounter any complication such as tiredness or physical exhaustion, and there is no need to compensate for energy from natural and other resources.

In addition, a "**Protective Layer**" (more details on page 123) shields the Fara-therapist from the dangers of the **Emitted Defective Cellular Consciousness** and other negative emissions of the patient, and from Non-organic Beings[3].

For the patient, treatment serves as a mystical (*Erfan*-based) journey for his **spiritual transformation**, because in this doctrine, physical healing without a constructive inner evolution fails to deliver the necessary values. Patient's linkage to the Interuniversal Divine Consciousness directs his attention toward an intel-

---

3- The term "Non-organic Beings" is applied to beings that are void of any organic or material aspect, whose unidentified form is not amassed with any atoms or molecules. According to the "Non-organic Viruses Theory" mankind is encountered with viruses that could affect his mind, body and psyche; infiltrate in man's diverse existing components and data files, having them contaminated with parasites and derangement. For details on Non-organic Viruses please refer to the book Non-organic Beings, by the same author.

ligent source and establishes the grounds for inner spiritual awakening.

Oh thou Saki (wine server in Farsi)! Give me a glass from that spiritual wine,

So that I could rest a moment from this corporeal veil.

-Sheikh Bahai

Very Important Note: Age, gender, level of education, studies, knowledge, spiritual and different mental experiences and trainings, personal abilities and talents, the type and style of nutrition, physical exercise, rigorous self-discipline and abstinence, and so on have absolutely no effect on interacting with the Interuniversal Consciousness. The reason for this independence is that *Ettesal* and its benefits are indeed **Divine Communal Mercy** and Grace, which embraces everybody without any exception.

Behold'. Last night a messenger from the invisible world

Gave the delightful news while I was drunk (spiritual ecstasy);

"His blessing is all-encompassing"

-Hafez

In this doctrine the individual [Fara-therapist] is completely disarmed from his personal abilities and talents, and carries out the therapy without possessing any means or method that he could attribute to himself. The treatment is only carried out via the linkage of *Ettesal*, which has been passed on and entrusted to him along with the protective layer. Accordingly; in this therapy no type of concentration, imagination and visualization, mantra and chanting, drawing any symbols and signs, prompting suggestions and inculcation, self-hypnosis methods and so on are not used.

In *Faradarmani* doctrine it is believed that the individual is able to benefit from an immense amount of spiritual competence through *Ettesal*, part of which is the ability to heal. It can also help the individual discover his inner treasures and reach the state of **enlightenment**, meaning clear-sightedness and spiritual insight and illumination, clarity of vision about existence, and understanding of the universe. It also facilitates the basis for transcendence of both the **individual's soul** and the **collective soul** of the society, which in turn elevates the human being's [level of awareness] and reduces his pain and suffering.

Man -the noblest of noble creatures, for his creation of which God glorified Himself- is not worthy of pain and illness. Thus, the effort to free himself from pain and suffering and humiliation not only causes no negative **Karma** (reaction), but also is a part of man's mission, especially because a number of pains and illnesses are as a result of life style, mental attitude, false beliefs, and, most important of all, falling away from Divine (Communal) Mercy.

In this discipline, all attainments occur only through the aid of *Halqehs* of His Communal Grace, and without this there is nothing one can do. In this regard, one is completely disarmed and under no circumstances can he do anything that would credit the treatment and healing to the Fara-therapist. Therefore, in *Faradarmani* there is no need for chanting and mantra, imagination and visualization, drawing any symbols and signs, prompting suggestions, self- hypnosis, and so on. The proof is very simple, as everybody can observe that without the use of the above-mentioned methods, the treatment still occurs and in this respect nothing can be added to *Faradarmani*.

There is a possibility that some people intend to establish new branches or methods for themselves by adding formalities and rituals, gestures and sentences, partial or whole definitions, or by denouncing one or several principles of Faradarmani. Nevertheless, by omitting and disregarding such definitions or insertions, we can well observe that Faradarmani continues to be effective as it ever was, and despite the applied alterations, the fundamentals of the subject still remain intact. Therefore, this test is the best means of uncovering and identifying the deceivers, those who manipulate and make alterations in the original concept, and the opportunists. Those will be forever indebted, and their action as a breach of trust and betrayal of what has been entrusted to them, will always reveal their disgrace apart from its spiritual consequences.

In *Faradarmani* the Fara-therapist and patient benefit from the Divine Communal Mercy and achieve a cure only through *Ettesal* (linkage) and by surrendering to the Interuniversal Consciousness, and they merely play the role of an **impartial observer.**

Drink from this wine and let your heart become an observer (of His beauty)

As His beauty is not dependent on embellishments

-Hafez

Consciousness is neither visible nor measurable; therefore, we can only observe its manifestations in the body, and then study or report them. The individual remains only as an impartial observer throughout the *Ettesal* (link) to observe what the consciousness is implementing in him, therefore he does not interfere at all with the Scanning procedure. For example, somebody with a gastric ulcer should not draw all his attention only toward his stomach, because his illness might be psychosomatic, and the *Interuniversal Consciousness* based on its discretion may start the Scanning process from his psyche. Therefore one must not impose his own idea, or interfere, and must not direct his attention merely to the pain and the painful area.

Through this path, a fortunate experience happens which we call "**omission of the self**" wherein one puts himself aside and avoids manifestations of **egocentricity**. This could be an introductory practice for experiencing selflessness and omission of the self, because we are always used to interfering and are not used to remaining only as an observer. To ensure that we are completely benefitting from the *Interuniversal Consciousness*, and that it is only the *Interuniversal Consciousness* at work, we must set aside all our personal skills and techniques and remain only an **impartial** observer of the *Faradarmani* processes.

Everything man attains through these *Halqeh*es is considered as man's "**Heavenly daily portion**," and he can also make a donation to others and share it with them ("...and spend out of what We have provided for them" -Quran; Baqarah: 3)

In *Faradarmani* one goes through an *Erfan*-based spiritual journey; therefore, one encounters matters that have their own special language [both in terminology and unlocking the secrets] and are discussed in theory and proved in practice.

The final conclusion is that Faradarmani is not the destination, but is a means of self-exploration, and the main purpose is to reach Kamal and personal transformation.

Interuniversalism

Interuniversalism is a totally meta-holistic way of viewing the human being. It is completely *Erfan*-based in that man is not considered as just a pile of flesh and bones but as vast as the universe:

The man became the universe,

the universe became man.

There is not a word more refined than that.

-Sheikh Mahmoud Shabestari

On the face (physical form), you are the microcosm. But in essence, you are the macrocosm.

-Molana Rumi

According to this view, the human being consists of several bodies such as the **physical body, psycheal body (psyche), mental body (Zehn, Mind), astral body,** and others. It also consists of:

• Several energy transformers, called
"chakras."

• Different energy channels such as the fourteen confined an blocked channels which are considered in acupuncture.

• Different energy fields around the body such as the polarity fiel and field of bio-plasma.

• Other components like cellular intelligence, molecular frequency, and endless other unknown parts.

In *Interuniversalism*, each cell is studied in relation to other cells. **Body, psyche, Zehn** and other bodies are in connection and communication with one another, denoting that that damage to any of these constituents, also disturbs the others. Having such an outlook on a human being makes identifying his illnesses and defective areas almost impossible.

Generally, until now, the treatments have been such that each discipline and intellectual method has examined the human merely from a particular angle. In doing so, each discipline has identified the defects only from one point of view, and has thus defined the illness and the treatment accordingly.

For example **conventional medicine** has considered the human as a machine and has focused only on the physical body: flesh, bone and skin. Likewise, **homeopathy** has focused only on cellular intelligence, **polarity therapy** only on polarity fields, **cymatic therapy**[4]" on molecular frequency, and so on; Each has viewed the human being from their own special perspective and has offered a uni-dimensional definition of the human being, examining only a certain aspect of him.

Accordingly, the story of the human being is similar to that of *Molana Rumi*'s Elephant in the darkness. In this story, a group of people stumble upon an elephant in the darkness, not knowing what they have run into. The one who touches the elephant's leg, identifies the elephant as a pillar. Someone who touches the back of the elephant identifies him as a cushion. The one who touches the elephant's ear identifies him as a fan, and so on. The story of man is the same.

The one who has examined his flesh and bone, only relates his illnesses to the malfunction of these parts. One who relates to cellular intelligence declares illness happens when cellular intelligence is defective, and the one who studies chakras, says illness happens when the chakras are out of balance. The opinion of someone who understands acupuncture is that illness happens when the energy in each of the 14 channels is imbalanced or blocked. In cymatic therapy, illness is defined as a conflict in the molecular frequency. Polarity healers believe illness happens when the fields of polarity are disturbed. People who have studied the human aura only view the illness in this way and seek merely to correct the aura. Finally, what is the all-inclusive and accurate definition of illness?

According to Interuniversalism theory, the definition of illness is: **"Any disorder, obstruction, damage, and imbalance in any of the infinite elements and components of the human being."**

If we accept this definition and apply it, we realize that it is impossible for mankind to be able to identify their own illnesses. One of the reasons for the plu-

---

4- Cymatic therapy is a controversial complementary medical technique using acoustic waves which was developed in the 1960s by Sir Peter Guy Manners. It is based on the assumption that human cells, organs, and tissues have each a natural resonant frequency which changes when perturbed by illness.

rality of branches of treatment is that treatment has to become feasible and accomplishable for the therapist, and for this purpose, one branch has been divided as much as possible into several specialized sub-branches in order to facilitate the diagnosis and its accuracy. Nevertheless, many diagnoses are still incorrect.

In *Faradarmani*, the patient is treated according to the definition of illness proposed by **Interuniversalism**. Contrary to all treatment methods in which the diagnosis and treatment of illnesses are carried out by human and the therapist has the crucial role, in *Faradarmani* this role is independent of human interventions, and only a great consciousness has the crucial role of **searching and Scanning** the patient, diagnosing the defective constituents, and performing their treatment.

The Scanning inspects the individual's whole being which, as we explained before, encompasses countless different constituents. Accomplishing this task is not possible without the help of a grand intelligence beyond the wisdom, expertise, and knowledge of human beings.

The Fara-therapist is disarmed of all his individual abilities for two reasons:

1. In order to prove the existence of such supreme consciousness (as discussed above, the *Interuniversal Consciousness*). In a way that after accomplishing the treatment, the Fara-therapist becomes certain that except for the Divine intelligence, there have been no other phenomena involved throughout the entire process. Therefore, this belief and certainty leads him to the owner of this intelligence, that is, God. In this way he gets to know God in practice:

Look clearly, because the light which you call the "moonlight" is indeed the "sunshine."

(Because the moon does not have any light on its own,

it merely reflects the light it receives from the Sun.)

-Shah Nemat-Allah Vali

We are drunk and wrecked in the wine house.

Bless this sweet drunk.

The mirror is lighted up by His radiance.

By looking at the moon, find a clue to the sunshine.

-Shah Nemat-Allah Vali

2. Surrendering, entrusting, and giving up effort and struggle in spiritual matters and divine affairs, and in circles (*Halqeh*) of His grace.

Never can you reach the jewel of the desire by own endeavor.

It's mere delusion to do this without intermediary (Divine help)

–Hafez

Furthermore, no formal statement of declaring one's intention is needed for performing *Faradarmani*.

The chalice revealing the universe (Jam-e-Jam),

is the luminance essence of the Friend (God).

Expressing a need in such a place, is not necessary [as he clearly

knows everything]

-Hafez

The law for spiritual affairs: surrender and submission.

The law of worldly affairs: effort and endeavor.

("That man can have nothing but what he strives for" - Quran; Najm: 39)

("And strive and endeavor in His path" - Quran; Ma-ida: 35)

("And strive and struggle, with your possessions and your lives, on the path of God" - Quran; Taubah: 41)

Therefore, in addition to providing the possibility of treatment, *Faradarmani* leads us towards a practical theism (empirical *Erfan*). Now we continue to further discuss the *Interuniversal Consciousness*:

In Interuniversal Mysticism (*Erfan-e Halqeh*), the *Interuniversal Consciousness* is defined as the awareness and consciousness governing the material world. As you can see in (Figure13), there are a number of *Halqeh*es available linked (*Ettesal*) to this network, one of which is *Faradarmani*, the one that is being considered and studied in this book.

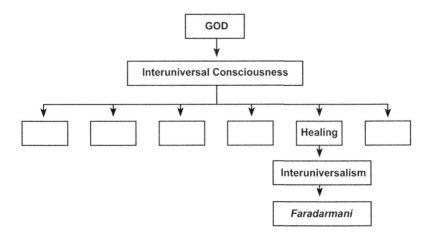

Each *Halqeh* of *Interuniversal Consciousness* provides us a special facility, and in *Interuniversal Mysticism* with the aid of such *Halqehes*, one can travel the spiritual journey of *Erfan* and self-exploration.

(Figur_13)

Man, Illness, and Transformation

Fighting illness is among the most significant challenges of man throughout his lifetime on Earth, and the dream of overcoming illness has formed one of his greatest wishes.

Human beings have always thought that if there were no illnesses, they could taste the sweetness of happiness and at least for moments live in peace. However, if humans were not struggling with the hindrance of illnesses, could they really reach such happiness, peace and prosperity? Without a doubt, our answer to this important question is "No". The reason is that with a little attention, one can see that the factor impeding man from reaching happiness, peace, and prosperity is not the illness, but man himself; his own poisonous being has been always used against him.

When I talk about the evil, I mean myself,

Because I have not seen a poison like "self" in the whole universe.

The enemy of my life, is no one except "me" that I am moaning of,

I would like to burn like the woods in the fire (to become free) from this self.

-Molana Rumi

Hafez! You, yourself, are the veil getting in the way. Arise from this midst and go away.

Blessed he who can go through the path with no veil.

-Hafez

Because the major enemy of human being and the veil that conceals his happiness is his own being, even by eliminating illnesses his problems will not be solved, and may even increase. The reason is that the illness itself serves as an effective factor in preventing man's extravagant ambitions and his unruliness, the very ambitions that dragged the egocentric human being to destruction and devastation.

If Pharaoh were in illness and pain,

That rebellious man would not dare to do such claims (of being God)

-Molana Rumi

Consequently, we can understand that the treatment of illnesses is not the way to salvation and freedom for the lost human being. He needs something beyond treatment, a source that can transform, and free him from himself, a positive change toward *Kamal*; and without such radical change, human beings will always live in devastation.

In order to materialize this ideal, we view man and his problems from a new perspective and we consider and analyze every possible solution for transforming him. Accordingly we discover that solutions outside such perspective will not have much effect in creating a radical positive change.

Therefore, in this doctrine, treatment is merely a means for creating such transformation for both the Fara-therapist and the patient. *Faradarmani* is an *Erfan*-based path for reaching much higher purposes, which, in addition to treatment, creates a ground for mental transformation and changes of perspective. This method, in addition to treating the patient, directs his attention toward a conscious source, an eternal consciousness which in turn establishes a basis for a transcendental inner transformation; man's problem is that he is not familiar with such a source in practice.

Faradarmani is capable of providing such experience for the patient in a manner that, while he observes the process of treatment taking place intelligently and without the interference of any material factor or any attempt based upon the expertise and knowledge of humans, he is subconsciously exposed to an enormous power. Eventually this can lead him to the perception of this conscious source, and the necessary subsequent changes in his perspective will follow. Therefore, it is extremely important to ensure that the originality of the above mentioned insight must be preserved so that the individual merely connects to the *Interuniversal Consciousness*.

To achieve this goal, the simultaneous interference of complementary treatments must be avoided, such as herbal medicine, phlebotomy, massage therapy, homeopathy, and any other unconventional treatment that might distract the patient's mind from the Divine intelligence. This not only saves the patient from confusion, but also prevents him from continuing the same manner of thinking and keeping the same perspectives. Otherwise, the simultaneous interference of complementary treatments not only undermines the magnificence and glory of *Interuniversal Consciousness*, and deprives the patient from accessing the pure and salvaging awareness, but also brings about conflict and disorder for the Fara-therapist.

Saki! Come, as the invisible messenger uttered to me glad tidings, "While in pain, exercise patience, for the remedy of union, I will send thee."

-Hafez

When the *Ettesal* (link) to the *Interuniversal Consciousness* is in operation, human-prescribed instructions are nothing but a desire to show off and it causes nothing but disturbance.

Definition of Ettesal

In *Faradarmani* the meaning of *Ettesal* is establishing a form of connection or link for which there is no accurate definition, because it occurs in a world that is Free of Tool, and we can study only the effects and influences of *Ettesal*, but not the nature of *Ettesal* itself.

Establishing Ettesal

- **Principle:** In order to benefit from the practical part of *Interunversal Mysticism* (*Erfan-e Halqeh*), we need to establish *Ettesal* to the various *Halqeh*es of the *Interuniversal Consciousness*.

These ***Ettesals*** **are the inseparable essentials of this branch of** ***Erfan*,** **and in order to fulfill each concept of this doctrine in practice, we need a specific** ***Halqeh*** **and its related special "Shield."** *Ettesal* **is given to both groups, the students and the instructors (masters), by means of entrusting, granting, agreeing with and signing the related text of oath. This entrusting is carried out by a centrality which controls and directs the affairs of the** ***Interuniversal Mysticism*.**

Principle: There are two general types of *Ettesal* to

the Interunivesal Consciousness:

A-Individually or personal type ("And your Lord says: "Call on Me Od'uni); I will answer your (prayer)"- Quran; Ghafir: 60)

In the personal type, a person, by means of his extraordinary, and prodigious eagerness and enthusiasm (*Eshtiyaq*), without the help of an instructor or guide, becomes connected to the *Interuniversal Consciousness*. To establish such an *Ettesal*, an prodigious *Eshtiyaq* is necessary. Otherwise, there is no definition for this way of *Ettesal*. (Figure 14 A)

The moment Hafez wrote this scribble of poetry,

The bird of his thought (logic), had fallen into the trap of longing and

Eshtiyaq.

-Hafez

B-Collective or common type ("And hold fast, all together, by the Rope (bond) which God (stretches out for you), and be not divided among yourselves" -Quran; Al-e-Emran: 103)

In the common way, with the assistance of an individual who serves as a connector, one becomes present in the Circle (*Halqeh*) of Unity. Every *Halqeh*, as shown in Figure 14 B, has three members: the *Interuniversal Consciousness*, the person who serves as a connector [Me], and the person who is about to be connected [You].

Upon the formation of the *Halqeh*, **Divine grace** immediately flows through it, and in the scope of this *Erfan*, the necessary actions will be taken through different *Halqeh*es. For a *Halqeh* to be formed the presence of the aforementioned three members is sufficient; in such cases, the fourth member will be **Allah or God (The Creator)**.

In *Erfan-e Halqeh Ettesal* is established based on the common or collective way in which the Divine grace flows through. The formation of this *Halqeh* is illustrated in Figure 14 B.

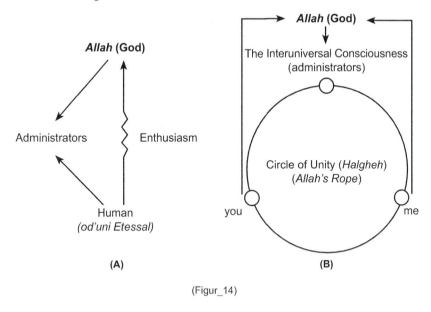

(A)   (B)

(Figur_14)

In the world of *Erfan*, the *Halqeh* of Unity has been repeatedly mentioned with different names and descriptions. For example, *Saadi* says:

The alluring chain of the Beloved's hair is formed of Halqeh's, which keep away the troubles.

The one out of this chain (Halqeh),

(That is not connected to the Beloved through this chain)

Is disengaged from all these ventures.

Saadi, in addition to stating the existence of *Halqehs*, also points out that whoever is not within these circles will be deprived of the blessings that flow through them. He also clearly points out that unless an individual unites in *Halqeh* with [at least] another individual, nothing will be shown to him.

Whoever is not aggregated (with someone else)

Can't go sightseeing (observing).

Friends travel together not alone.

-Saadi

Hafez points out that anybody who is interested in communication with God will never step out of this *Halqeh* which is indeed the *Halqeh* of *Ettesal*.

The one who seeds desire and dream of the green (delightful) path of Your residence,

Won't step out of this circle; as long as he is alive.

Molana Rumi has talked about the Ettesal between human beings and God:

A simple measureless Ettesal, is between the God of people and the heart of people,

An Ettesal, which words can't bear,

But its utterance is a "must,"

That's all I have to say.

Hafez likens *Ettesal* to drinking wine from the wine-server's cup and considers it illuminating and *Kamal*-attaining:

Come Saki! With the wine that elicits ecstasy,

Increases blessings, and heightens (the level of my) Kamal.

Give me some, for I am shattered of love.

I have lost my heart and from these both been deprived.

And another poet adds:

Come Saki! With that wineglass that purifies,

Which opens one's heart to insights.

Give me some for it can bring me inner serenity,

And pull me out of the unhappiness and darkness for a second.

Upon becoming present in the *Halqeh* of Unity and establishing *Ettesal*, the Divine grace runs through which the mystics have likened to drinking wine. The wine from His wine-jar of awareness and insight runs into man's soul and, in addition to creating spiritual joyfulness and intoxication, also pours knowledge, awareness, insight, and love. In mystic language God is called "The Server" (**Saki**) of wine.

Oh thou Saki! Give me a glass from that spiritual wine,

So that I could rest a moment from this corporeal veil.

-Sheikh Bahai

Molana Rumi, has written about this *Ettesal*, drinking from the wine jar of the Divine unity, and its comparison with worldly wine, as follows:

Thou wine server of the soul, please fill up my cup again.

That bandit of the heart that takes my religion away and shows me the true religion.

From the wine which springs from the heart and merges with the soul

Its bubbles make languishing, every truth-seeking eye.

(This wine changes the way you perceive things, in a way that enables you to see the truth behind the surface, which in turn brings ecstasy)

That wine of grape, the bodily wine,

And this wine of God, the heavenly downpour.

There are plenty of jars filled with each type of wine.

Unless you break "that" one, you can't taste "this" one

"That" empties you from your sorrows for only a minute or so

But kills not the sorrowfulness,

And never takes out the roots of hostility and hatred.

Whilst a sip from "this" wine, makes your universe golden.

I give my life for "this" golden wine.

And finally...

Oh how empty the goblet of my body,

Wine, how pure a wine in Saki's hands.

So thou the wine server of souls pour wine

into the goblet of my heart and soul.

From the jar of your wisdom and awareness,

Your knowledge, oneness, and Eshq.

-*Mohammad Ali Taheri*

The blessing which flows in the *Halqeh* of Unity is a result of the closeness and unity of a minimum of two people, and anywhere that at least two people come together in this *Halqeh*, the third member is the Holy Spirit, and the fourth is God.

The only condition for becoming present in the *Halqeh* of Unity is to be an impartial observer or spectator, that is, a witness who observes all the occurrences during his presence in the *Halqeh* without any pre-assumption, interpretation, or judgment (saves all contemplations and interpretations for when he comes out of the *Halqeh*), and keeps everything that happens under observation.

Nobody has the right to introduce this *Ettesal* in any name other than the *Interuniversal Consciousness* or Divine Consciousness; otherwise, it is considered as deception, deviating people from the way to God, and misleading them toward **"anything other than God or instead of Him"**. (The principle of avoiding *Min Dun-e-Allah* or anything other than God or instead of Him; is taken from the Quran.) In this regard, anything that one may use to promote and propound himself or anything that leads to egocentricity and claiming superiority over others is a blatant deviation. (The principal of avoiding **"I am better than him"**[5]; taken from the Quran; Al-Araf: 12).

It has become evident from the above explanations that *Faradarmani* therapy is not performed by the Fara-therapist but is actually carried out by *Ettesal* to the *Interuniversal Consciousness*. The Fara-therapist only plays the role of a member who helps to create a **Halqeh of Unity** that provides the flow of Divine Communal Mercy.

Therefore, therapy is not dependent on the energy, skill or expertise of the Fara-therapist, as it is performed by an intelligence much higher than any human intelligence. The skill or talent of the Fara-therapist has no influence on the treatment results. In this way, the Fara-therapist does not encounter any kind of physical side effect such as exhaustion or physical strain, and so there is no need for any kind of energy "recharge" from nature or other resources.

The essential condition for entering this *Halqeh* is submission or surrendering which is equivalent to being an impartial observer which will be discussed separately.

The Principles of Human Being's Communication with God

•Principle: When man has a request from God he directly

asks Him. *Iyaaka Nastaien*: We ask help (for each and everything) only (and absolutely) from You (Quran; *Faatihah*: 5)

("Muhammad! Say thou: 'I am but a man like you: it is revealed to me by revelation, that your God is One God, so stand true to Him, and ask for God's forgiveness, and woe to polytheists, those who join gods with God." -Quran; Fussilat: 6) (Those who violate the principle of "going directly to Him")

But man's request will be answered through Divine Intelligence, or by conven-

---

5- Allah asked [Satan]: 'what prevented you to prostrate [to man], when I commanded you?' ''I am better than he (man)," Satan replied. 'You created me of fire and you created him of clay.'

Egocentricity and sense of superiority over others is rooted in the Negative Network (Chapter 4) and its origin in Creation dates back to the Satan's sense of superiority over man. Therefore, man should learn from this and not forget that selfishness is the factor causing disobedience and rebellion against God's will. Egocentricity, including all types of power display or dominance, distances man from his Kamal-seeking mission.

tion the *Interuniversal Consciousness* (*"God does not talk to any human except through direct revelation (inspiration), or through a barrier (veil), or by sending a messenger which would convey the message with God's permission."* -Quran; *Shura: 51*) And no man is exempted from this rule, as anyone who is called a human being, according to the figure below, holds the same aforementioned position. Also, if the "human" label is removed from somebody, such an entity is considered as a "being" other than human, and he will not be in this category, and his *Kamal* will be considered and discussed outside the scope of human being's *Kamal*. Otherwise, not only would the holy verses above be refuted, but Divine justice regarding the equality of all human beings before God would also be questioned.

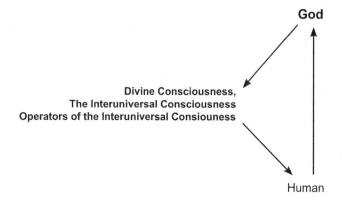

Submission in heavenly (spiritual) matters and endeavor in worldly (material) matters are determining factors in a human being's life. Worldly matters, in turn, are dependents of both free will and pre-destination.

In general, predestination is the factor that has made the dipolar world not predictable or calculable, and so has given meaning to the whyness of a human being's progress (journey). If this were not the case, all events would have been predictable and foreseeable, there would be no need for decision making and human's free will, man's progress would have been completely meaningless, and the whyness of the human beings' creation nullified. In *Erfan-e Halqeh*, human-related factors such as all personal characteristics, geographical and regional conditions, individual capabilities and resources and so on, have no role in establishing *Ettesal* and receiving metaphysical and spiritual awareness. Therefore, the following factors have absolutely no influence on benefiting from the network of *Interuniversal Consciousness*, and receiving its awareness [inspiration and revelation].

• Gender, age, nationality, talent, education, knowledge, ideology, be liefs, mystical and spiritual experience, and so on.

• Strenuous self-discipline, physical exercise, type of nutrition, and so on.

• Endeavour, effort, struggle, determination, and so on.

• Imagination and mental visualization, mantra and chanting, using signs and symbols, prompting suggestion, inculcation and repetition, concentration, and so on.

Type of an individual's morphology such as *Damavi(Sanguine)*, *Bal ghami(Phelgmatic)*, *Sodaie (Atrabilious)* and *Safravi (Bilious)* types; or *Vata*, *Pita*, *Kafa*, and so on.

Definition of Impartial Observer and Surrendering

An impartial observer is someone who:

• Observes and is witnessing.

• Does not let anything such as imagination, visualization and inter pretation interfere with his observation, as this would prevent him from impartial witnessing.

• Is able to see the reality and the truth [Coin of Existence].

• Is without any bias, judgment and pre-assumption.

• Is present in the moment.

• Has not been conditioned.

• Is free (no use of hallucinogens).

• Is surrendering (not doing anything else in the *Halqeh* except for observing).

There is nothing better than trust in God,

Nothing is more favorable than surrendering.

-Molana Rumi

The only condition for becoming present in the *Halqeh* of Unity is being an impartial observer. An impartial observer is one who is observing and witnessing. While observing; he is free from any pre-judgments or pre-conceptions, and he witnesses each and every occurrence in the *Halqeh* and refrains from any interpretations and deductions during this time (any interpretation or deduction must be after the *Ettesal* and not during it). The only condition for the *Halqeh* to take place is through submission.

Definition of the Protective Layer or Shield

The Protective Layer (Shield) is made of consciousness and is entrusted upon the Fara-therapist after completing the written oath. This layer, under the control of Interuniversal Consciousness, protects the Fara-therapist and also provides the patient with a confident shield during *Faradarmani* (in both short and long-distance Faradarmani). This is to protect the Fara-therapist and the patient against **the "interference of faulty cellular consciousness," "negative emissions," and particularly against the penetration of "Non-organic Beings."**

(Figure 15)

The main language of human beings is the language of "emission"; likely to have been well experienced by most of us; for example, if we sit next to a depressed individual, even without knowing him or talking to him, we will also have a feeling of heaviness and lassitude after a very short time. Indeed as the [Persian] proverb goes, "the disheartened soul disheartens the company." In contrast, if we sit in the vicinity of a happy and cheerful individual, after a while we will also feel cheerful and high-spirited. Upon encountering certain people, we feel relaxed but with others we may feel anxious.

Psychologists and people who must interact with psychologically disordered individuals, and must concentrate on them for considerably long periods of time, are to a greater extent subject to the interference of negative emissions and other interferences; consequently, the patient's negative nervous habits (tics) can be transferred to them through emissions. Others who, due to their profession, have to sit with clients, listen to them and concentrate for a long time are more likely subject to such contamination than those who do not. Lawyers, hypnotherapists, and counselors are among the more at-risk group. According to *Faradarmani*, one type of contamination is **"Emission-based Contamination."**

Important Note: Once the text of the oath is written, the Fara-therapist-to-be appoints a time for receiving the protective layer and announces it to his instructor (*Faradarmani* master); then the master announces this to *Interuniversal Consciousness*. The position of the individual from the standpoint of geographical direction, body position such as sitting, standing, lying down, remaining still or moving, and so on, have no effect on receiving the protective layer and even if the receiver forgets to undertake the relevant *Ettesal* [on the pre-arranged time], the protective layer will still be received.

The protective layer of each individual is as unique as their fingerprint and the form and manner of it being carried out, is unique for each person, hence there is no possibility for two people having identical protective layers.

Faradarmani

Upon applying *Faradarmani*, the **Fara-therapist**, by connecting (*Ettesal*) the patient to the *Interuniversal Consciousness*, exposes him to *Interuniversal Consciousness* for treatment to take place in accordance with the aforementioned explanations. In this case, the patient is called a *Faradarmani* receiver. A **Faradarmani Clinic** is a specialized place in which *Faradarmani* is practiced.

The Purpose of [Practicing] Faradarmani

Faradarmani, as an *Erfan*-based practice, is applied by a Fara-therapist for achieving the following objectives:

1.Practical Acquaintance with Divine Intelligence (The Interuniversal Consciousness) and Practical Theology or Theism in Practice.

By applying *Faradarmani* in practice, the intelligence and consciousness governing the universe is proved in practice, and following that, the question will be raised about the source of the *The Interuniversal Consciousness*. Therefore, we have to say this *Consciousness* in turn has come from somewhere or has a source or owner that we call "God or the Creator"; in fact, we want to discover the cause through the effect:

Look clearly,

Because the light which you call the "moonlight"

Is indeed the "sunshine."

-Shah Nemat-Allah Vali

By seeing the moonlight, we are led to the main source providing the light, the Sun. Although we cannot bear to look at the Sun for long, we can look at the moonlight with no concern and enjoy its light.

2.Becoming Free From Being A Captive Of "Self"

One of the greatest problems of human beings is the prison of 'self' or being imprisoned within oneself. Everybody constantly thinks and talks about their own problems; however, if somebody else wants to talk about his problem, he is told that it is "his" problem and it does not concern others. This is how a human being has been trapped in the prison of 'self' and has become imprisoned in a futile circle. The entangled human being cannot comprehend the truths of the universe around him when he is confined in the fort of self.

If you get so engaged, entangled in Self,

This self of you will be a veil,

Imprisoning you from the surrounding universe.

-Sheik Mahmoud Shabestari

Therefore, in this branch of *Erfan*, therapy serves as a means for becoming separated from the self. As the Fara-therapist inquires and understands the problems of others, he will come out of himself; and after gaining this experience, he becomes aware of the beautiful and pleasant surroundings that also exist outside his fort, and realizes that he has been imprisoned in such a fort in vain.

You won't gird your waist with such a tight binding belt,

If you see that the one in the midst (who becomes squashed)

Is nobody but yourself.

-Hafez

As long as you are engaged in your knowledge and superiority, you are void of wisdom indeed.

I just tell you one tip, do not see self;

From then on, you are freed.

-Hafez

3. To Attain Practical Worship

There are two kinds of worships: **Theoretical** or verbal worship and **Practical** worship. For better understanding of this concept, we compare worship to friendship, which also has verbal and practical aspects. In its verbal form, utterance (of the tongue) is the determining factor to such a degree that, in words, one may even give his life for others [having a smooth tongue]! Such flattery shows that we are at the service of others. But once someone is in trouble, those who were verbally devotees and companions leave the stage of action by bringing up all kinds of excuses. After all, how can we count on somebody's friendship? Definitely, when they stay by our sides in difficult times, indeed, this could be the proof of real friendship.

This principle also implies to practical worship. Addressing God we say *"Al-Hamdu Lillah,"* praise belongs to *Allah* (God) and all gratitude is reserved for Him, *"Subhan Allah,"* God is All-Pure, and other tokens of flattery. But how can Heaven count on our words? That is when our sweet-talks are accompanied by our actions, and our actions confirm our words. Therefore, **"Come! Towards the best of deeds"**[6]is the ultimate factor determining our friendship with the higher world. Otherwise, flattering words are easy to utter, and everybody can do so. **"Friendship in Practice"** is a guarantee for **"Verbal Friendship,"** and without the practice, although verbal friendship is sweet and pleasant, it holds no value.

However, when a human being intends to attain practical friendship with regard to God, he finds out that God is by no means in need of any of our services and He is the absolute "Free of Need."

Such imperfect love as ours,

The Beloved magnificence has no need.

For the perfect beauty,

Is not in need of frills and adornment.

-Hafez"

So what should we do?

We can say that all man's positive deeds must be focused on 'manifestations' of God; which is indeed the entire universe. Subsequently, our practical services must also embrace human beings as one of God's manifestations. Therefore, in the world of *Erfan*, it is said, "Worship is nothing but being at the service of people," and "Come! Toward the best of deeds."

Fasting all days, praying all nights

Every year setting off to Haj7,

Travelling as far as Hejaz8,

Sleepless all Friday nights (Muslim's common prayer night),

6- "Hayya Ala KhayrAI-Amal" Arabic phrase commonly used in Muslims prayers.

7- Haj is the name of Muslims' annual pilgrimage to Mecca, the Islamic holiest city where the "Kaaba" shrine is located.

8- Region in western Saudi Arabia, which is home to the Muslim holy cities of Mecca and Medina

Speaking of secrets to God,

And inquiring needs and desires,

From His free of need presence,

Becoming a hermit within all temples and Mosques,

Avoiding all prohibited acts, and unlawful pleasures9.

. From Medina to Kaaba, going with bare head and foot,

(exposing oneself to harsh conditions)

Opening the lips for answering the Labbaik10 to fulfill the duty,

I hereby swear (assure) none (of the above) could be as fruitful as, Opening a closed door (of hope) to a hopeless man.

-Sheikh Bahai

Following this explanation we discover that the blessing and opportunity of *Faradarmani*, that is now available and bestowed to us with the aid of Divine grace, is an appropriate means for attaining practical worship, and while helping others solve their problems, it also familiarizes them with Divine consciousness.

4. Recognition of the Inner Treasure

Man, in connection and *Ettesal* to the eternal Divine consciousness, can find the key for accessing the inner treasure of his existence, and subsequently increase his spiritual competence, and travel faster on the path of *Kamal.*

You are hidden from yourself,

If you finally find yourself,

The hidden treasure inside your soul will appear.

-Sheikh Attar

5. Providing A Way for Public Salvation

If a person wishes to only save himself, it is due to his selfishness and egocen-

---

9- Adapted from Shahriar Shahriari translation.

10- Part of Haj ceremony which entails saying to God: "I am at your service and have responded to your call."

tricity. On the contrary, one finds the way to God through saving others. In other words man's salvation is a collective (group) salvation. As *Ibne Arabi* says:

"When people become downcast and degraded in your sight, It is when Haqq (one of the names of God) has also of no importance to you."

Until all you are concerned is your own self,

You won't be forgiven.

Until self is with you,

Nothing will be revealed to you.

Until you are not free from yourself and both worlds, Don't knock this door Sir,

it won't be opened to you!

-Sheikh Mahmoud Shabestari

Whom you see gloomy and sad,

Is in love with his self affairs,

Let's not remark affairs of self,

And see affairs of others!

-Molana Rumi

Faradarmani Practice

For becoming a Fara-therapist, the relevant *Halqeh* is entrusted to the individual within one session. This is only after completing the corresponding written oath, pledging to make appropriate positive and humanitarian use of *Faradarmani*. After having written the oath, the ability of healing, together with its Protective Layer, is entrusted to the individual. Upon receiving the protective layer onward, he can immediately experience applying *Faradarmani* in its full capacity, in both short and long-distance treatments. However, it is necessary for him, in advance, to be fully aware of the aim and purposes of applying *Faradarmani*, and to realize that this is only for the purpose of gaining *Kamal*.

He must understand that applying *Faradarmani* for the purpose of gaining power is dangerous and will drag him into the Negative Network[11], so that he will turn into a selfish and egotistical human being who is only interested in showing off and self-aggrandizement. If he uses *Faradarmani* in this manner, the possibility of gaining insight as the final objective will be taken away from him. Therefore, it is highly recommended that the basic principles of *Faradarmani* treatment and the purposes of applying *Faradarmani* to be carefully studied or learnt from the masters. Before writing the Text of Oath, one should inquire about the necessary information on the matter from his master.

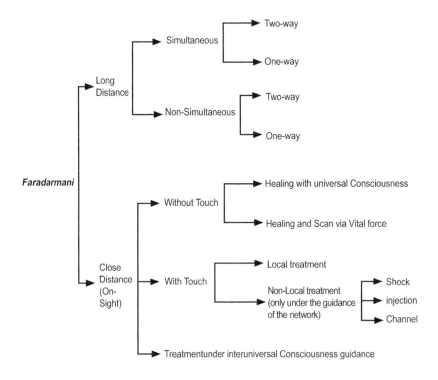

Important Note: *Faradarmani* cannot be attained through books, because it is an *Erfan*-based subject, and attaining practical *Erfan* (empirical *Erfan*) is not possible through books and writings; instead, it must be entrusted to the students through the masters.

11- For more details on The Negative Network please refer to chapter 4.

If you are our classmate, Wash white all the papers,

Scribbles in the books won't teach you the art of Eshq.

-Hafez

That silent spot is unutterable.

The first step is to forget all your books and learning.

-Sa'eb Tabriz

In general the objectives of *Faradarmani* course are:

•Theoretical acquaintance with the *Interuniversal Consciousness*, introduction to *Erfan* and the study of human [From a meta-holistic aspect including self-awareness, the philosophy of creation, and so on.]

•Practical acquaintance with the *Interuniversal Consciousness* through:

a. *Ettesal* to the Network and becoming exposed to Scanning process (treatment) for the purpose of:

-Diagnosis of the history of illnesses and areas of tension.

-Helping to restore physical, mental and psychological health.

-Elimination of involuntary movements and nervous habits.

-Increasing the amount of relaxation, concentration and peace.

b. Becoming a Fara-therapist and applying *Faradarmani* in practice, also receiving the protective shield for the purpose of providing the due safety and the necessary security during the therapy and while benefitting from the practical applications of connection to the *Interuniversal Consciousness*; against interference of emitted defective cellular consciousness and other environmental negative emissions, and the penetration of Non-organic Beings.

Different Types of Connection or Link between the Fara-therapist and the Patient in "Faradarmani"

In *Faradarmani* there are different types of links and methods of establishing a link with the patient which are categorized in the chart below. In *Faradarmani*, as mentioned before, treatment is possible from short and long distances. It is important to keep in mind that only authorized instructors must conduct the training; however, a brief description of different methods of establishing a link for patients to access *Ettesal* will be provided.

Long-Distance *Faradarmani*

The simplest type of *Faradarmani* is the long-distance treatment, which is done through *Ettesal* to the *Interuniversal Consciousness* and is possible in **simultaneous** and **non-simultaneous** mode.

A.Long Distance[12] Non-Simultaneous[13] *Faradarmani*

In this type of therapy, the Fara-therapist generally requires at least one specification of the patient. For example, knowing the patient's name, picture, face or the person who has introduced the patient (friend/family) is enough to begin the treatment.

In this case, the Fara-therapist enters the name of the patient or a reference corresponding to the patient's name[14] in the list of his patients, or he mentally reviews the name (this mental note is referred to as a "glance"[15] in *Erfan*). In this way, the patient is now [symbolically] registered in the Network of *Interuniversal Consciousness*, after which there is no need for further action by the Fara-therapist or the patient. The only condition required for treatment is that both sides must be in complete surrender and leave the treatment process to the network.

Any superfluous act is considered interference in the affairs of Divine intelligence and disturbs the [treatment] procedure. The less interference by both sides

---

12- Long-distance means that the Fara-therapist and the patient are physically distant and not in the presence of each other.

13- Non-simultaneous means that the patient has given us a time for his Ettesal in advance. For example he says that tomorrow night 10 O'clock I want to receive Faradarmani Ettesal, however in simultaneous connection, the patient calls or informs the Fara-therapist exactly at the time he wants to receive Faradarmani.

14- We may not personally know the patient, but considering the aforementioned specifications of the patient such as his name, picture, face or only the person who introduces the patient (his friend, family and so on), we can refer to the patient and in this way register him in the Network of Interuniversal Consciousness. For example we can say "Mr. X.; my neighbor's friend who is sick", while we do not even know the name of Mr. X.

15- NAZAR: or 'glance' is a fleeting moment of attention with the purpose of establishing a link to the Interuniversal Consciousness.

indicates a higher degree of surrendering, and thus facilitates the treatment. Not interfering, in itself, is the most difficult stage of working with the *Interuniversal Consciousness*. The reason is that human beings are instinctively inclined to achieve results through their own effort; therefore, they become confused when dealing with non-worldly [spiritual] matters, which are governed by the law of submission, where only surrender is meaningful and individual abilities have no place. Certainly with care and attentiveness it will all make sense to us, we can grasp this concept, and we will be able to easily benefit from Divine communal mercy.

Important Note: In both short and long-distance *Faradarmani* treatments the position or posture of the patient during the Scanning process via the *Interuniversal Consciousness* has no effect on the result of the treatment. **The patient can be lying down, standing up, or in any other position or direction.** It is also not necessary for the patient to close his eyes during the Scanning process, however it helps the patient to follow the Scanning process better and more easily; closing the eyes is especially recommended when the patient feels mentally distracted. The patient needs not to think about his illness, but he must keep observing his whole being during the process.

Important Note: Upon beginning the therapy, neither the patient nor the Fara-therapist are required any formal statement to engage in the therapy, because at that moment, both of them have been linked to the network and uttering anything is meaningless.

The cup, world displaying is the luminous mind of the Friend

There, is what need of revealing my own necessity?

-Hafez

Long-distance non-simultaneous treatment also has two forms:

I. Two way Non-simultaneous Faradarmani Link

In this type of connection, the patient has agreed to enter the Circle of Unity (*Halqeh*), and indeed has accepted to access treatment through the Interuniversal Consciousness, and is willing to establish a link (*Ettesal*) therefore, this type of connection is known as a two-way link.

In this case, in addition to their other specifications, it is necessary for the patient to announce a specific time or times within the 24-hour period to the Fara-therapist for establishing the *Ettesal*. The Fara-therapist must then review the appointed schedule once, as soon as possible, so that the patient's information becomes registered in the Interuniversal Network. This designates the beginning of the 24 hour *Ettesal* (link) which is considered as the general link for the patient. Additionally, the patient can establish a special link at the appointed time, which will allow them to experience and follow the Scanning process.

Other than announcing the list of his patients to the Interuniversal Network, the Fara-therapist is not required to do anything else; however, if he wants to, he can review the list daily (it is not essential and depends on the choice of the Fara-therapist). For example, the Fara-therapist announces the name of his patient to the network at seven o'clock in the morning (Figure 16), and the patient receives his link at ten o'clock at night (Figure 17). At this time, **the Fara-therapist may be busy doing something else and there is no need for him to accompany the patient in the link at the appointed time, nor is it necessary to do anything else in this regard.**

One of the reasons that the patient must specify a certain time for establishing the link is that this serves as a commitment for him to sit through the link, so that he can observe the events occurring during the course of treatment on him and feel the *Ettesal*. The connection begins at the designated time that the patient has announced [in this example 10 pm], but the ending is not certain and depends on the discretion of the Interuniversal Consciousness. If the process takes too long, after about 15 to 20 minutes, the patient can come out of the Scanning mode.

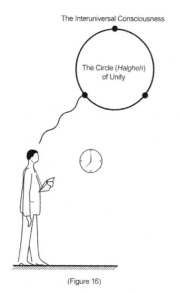

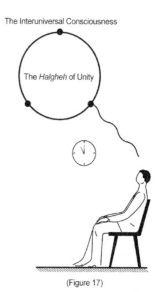

(Figure 16)   (Figure 17)

2. One-way Non-simultaneous Faradarmani Link

This type of connection is for those who have not announced their readiness for establishing a link through the *Interuniversal Consciousness* and have no cooperation with the Fara-therapist, but their friends and relatives want to help them by accessing treatment from the Interuniversal Consciousness.

The process for establishing this link is similar to that explained above, but with the difference that the patient does not have a specifically appointed time for the link, nevertheless only his name is announced to the *Interuniversal Consciousness* by the Fara-therapist [24 hours]. It is obvious that in such people the probability of recovery is less than with the two-way method.

B. Long-distance Simultaneous *Faradarmani*

This type of treatment uses technologies such as telephone and the Internet. In this method as in the short-distance treatment (see next page), [without physically doing anything] the Fara-therapist listens to the reports of the patient (which is optional) and follows up the process of treatment without the need of his physical presence. Another method is to establish the link by verbal agreement through a phone call, and then we hang up and obtain the patient's report about the treatment process at a more suitable time (Figure18).

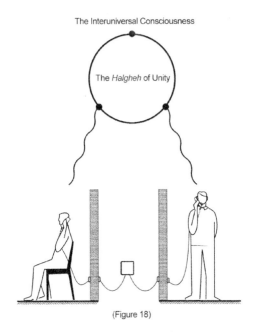

The Interuniversal Consciousness

The *Halgheh* of Unity

(Figure 18)

Short-Distance *Faradarmani*

In this type of treatment the patient and the Fara-therapist are in the presence of each other at one place [they visit each other in person]. As a general rule,

during a *Faradarmani* session the only thing the patient is required to do is to be an impartial observer, and follow the Scanning process through his body [Mind, psyche and so on]. In addition the Fara-therapist may wish to obtain a constant report on the occurrences and Scanning process from the patient. It is preferable that the patient follows the *Ettesal* with his eyes closed so that he can pay attention to the Scanning process more easily.

Short-distance *Faradarmani* treatment is divided into three categories:

1. Faradarmani without touch of the hand

This type of therapy, itself, is divided into the following sections:

1.Faradarmani and Scan through Interuniversal Consciousness

Scan via the *Interuniversal Consciousness* is the main procedure in Faradarmani. The main job of the Fara-therapist is to establish the link as mentioned earlier, and afterwards only listen to the patient's reports (optional) to follow up the treatment progress without the need of performing any physical action or doing anything in particular.

If the Fara-therapist chooses not to listen to the reports of the patient after the link (*Ettesal*) is established, he can leave the patient and follow up the results of the treatment at a more suitable time (Figure19).

(Figure 19)

2. Treatment and Scan through the Vital Force

This type of scan is applied when the Fara-therapist and the patient are at each other's presence [they visit each other]. In this method, the Fara-therapist holds the palm of his hands toward the patient, who also raises the palms of his hands toward the therapist. The distance between the Fara-therapist and patient is not important, and this procedure is appropriate only for short-distances [for long-distance there is no need for the hand position and the Vital Force scan takes place any way].

Then the patient can feel a kind of force (the Vital Force, see next page) entering through the palms of his hands and other parts of his body. When this current enters the patient's body, the Scan begins and the patient realizes that some actions are being carried out on various parts of his body; at this stage the Fara-therapist can acquire reports from the patient (optional). This type of scan yields the treatment for the patient and is called "**Scan with the Vital Force**" in *Faradarmani* (Figure 20).

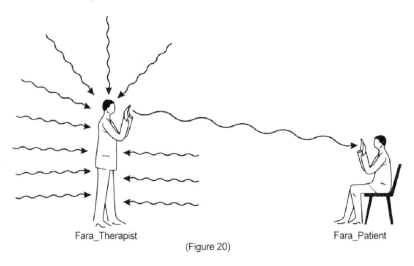

Fara_Therapist   Fara_Patient

(Figure 20)

Definition of Vital Force

The Vital Force is one of the subcategories of the *Interuniversal Consciousness,* and is derived from the Universal Consciousness and flows throughout the universe as a force. Within one session of *Faradarmani*, the ability to feel this force is entrusted [by the master] to the Fara-therapist, who, by moving his hand through the air, can feel this force and become conscious of the fact that we are immersed in it.

The Vital Force is like water that flows through a field, without which all of the vegetation would dry up and perish. Additionally, all vegetation benefits from this "water" regardless of their type or species. Thus, it becomes clear that all of existence has one common root and one common source of sustenance which is called the Vital Force.

Different disciplines employ this force by using imagination in a way that the individual imagines inhaling this force into his body and by guiding it to the various parts they are fortified by this force and the necessary actions are performed on them (as in yoga). Another example is by moving the hands through the air, as in tai chi, in which the individual imagines this force coming into contact with his hands and being absorbed into his body. But the problem with these methods is that after years of practice, once the individual says "I feel it", it is not clear whether this experience is imagined, induced through a conditioned response, or it is a true experience.

Concerning the fact that in *Faradarmani* no type of imagination or conditioning is authorized, so as to prevent individuals from being conditioned, such methods [such as tai chi and so on] are not utilized.

B. Faradarmani through Touch

1. Local (Topical) Treatment with the Touch of the Hand

After having written the text of the oath, one of the things entrusted to the Fara-therapist is performing localized *Faradarmani* through touch or by holding the painful area. The method is very simple and performed as follows. The Fara-therapist holds or touches the injured or aching location and asks the patient to report any local changes (optional); after a while, the patient reports a reduction in pain or improvement in the area.

2. Non-local Touch and Treatment

Another entrustment made to the Fara-therapist which gives a special quality to his hands, is the ability to apply shock, channel, and injection, each one with their own specific features. In this treatment the Fara-therapist holds a body part such as the patient's ankle, hand, arm, or ear, and then may request a report from the patient. Depending on the patient's needs, he will feel either a shock, or the formation of a channel, or a bar-shaped motion from the area the Fara-therapist's hands is located into the patient's body. The type of treatment which may be shock, channel, or injection, depends on the discretion of the *Interuniversal Consciousness* and the need of the patient; the choice cannot be made by the Fara-therapist [the Fara-therapist is a conduit for the treatment to take place by the Interuniversal Consciousness, and he is not in charge of the treatment].

For example, in patients who are in a coma, the Fara-therapist holds a limb or other body part, and a shock may be applied, after which the patient regains consciousness. Holding either the arm or leg of patients with motor dysfunction creates a channel from the place of contact to the brain or other limbs/organs, which is then followed by a positive report on the paralyzed organs. In some cases, the patient reports a rod-like movement or a current which is followed by pain, indicating that the injection has occurred, somewhat similar to the case of the channel but much more tangible [On the contrary to channels, injections come with pain].

Treatment Using the Body's Polarity Field (Polarity Therapy, Energy Therapy)

Concerning the fact that *Faradarmani* is neither Polarity nor Energy Therapy and there is no need to work with polarity field in Faradarmani, the following explanations are only provided for informational purposes. Polarity Therapy is performed by moving the hand within centimeters of the patient's body with the purpose of restoring the balance of the body's polarity field (Figure 22).

Description of the Polarity Force

The polarity field is one of the energy fields surrounding the human being and the body cells. Polarity means being polar, and the polarity field has positive and negative poles (Figure 21). This field is created by the ion and electron exchange of the body's one hundred trillion cells. In reality, there are several different currents that run through the human body, one of which is the electrical current. Therefore, according to the laws of physics, wherever an electrical current flows, there will also be a field surrounding that current. This field creates positively and negatively charged poles on each end.

It has been several decades since the human body's polarity field has been plotted and studied at a university in the United States, and today this subject is taught at different universities under the name of "Energy Therapy."[16] After the discovery of the polarity field in the USA, the names Polarity Therapy, Energy Therapy, and Force Therapy gained world-wide attention.

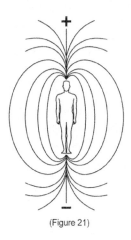

(Figure 21)

Polarity Therapy - Energy Therapy - Force Therapy

While conducting primary research on the human body's polarity field, researchers became aware that one of the causes of illness in humans could be related to a disturbance in this field. Following this research, it was noticed that by moving the hand within a few centimeters of the patient's body, the patient is exposed to the polarity field of the therapist's hand (Figure 22). This encounter results in a kind of movement or shift in the patient's polarity field, consequently the electron movement and ion exchange within his body will intensify, and if the illness is related to this, this action proves successful and leads to the improvement of the body's polarity field, which subsequently cures the illness.

16- http://www.polaritytherapy.org

Nevertheless, if the cause of illness is not related to a disturbance of this field, this action will obviously have no effect on the improvement of the patient's condition such as mechanical dysfunctions like arthritis, physical distortion, spinal injuries, and congenital disorders.

(Figure 22)

All human beings without exception possess polarity force, because the polarity field is part of every person's physical body; however some possess a more powerful field than others. Nevertheless in Faradarmani, once a link (*Ettesal*) is established through the Interuniversal Consciousness, with the correction of the ion and electron exchanges in the cells, the polarity field is automatically

corrected and it expands. Therefore, there is no need for correction through any hand movements.

Very Important Note: In Faradarmani, the Fara-therapist has no need to apply polarity therapy [with his hands as used in polarity therapy] because the polarity field will be automatically corrected wherever required through the *Ettesal* to the Interuniversal Consciousness. In short-distance treatment method, it is only the *Interuniversal Consciousness* that guides the treatment process, and the Fara-therapist is not in charge of choosing this method unless he wants to test it for his own experience.

Reasons for Disturbance in the Polarity Field

We will discuss several causes for this disturbance:

A)Effect of Technological Advancements

Technological advancements have created new circumstances in man's life, which disturb the environmental balance and create contamintions for human beings. These can be divided into several major categories.

A.1. Polarity Pollution

•Polarity Pollution Caused by Metals

Examples include: living in buildings constructed with metal frameworks, using metal objects, using cars, and so on. The metals create a field around themselves and when coming into contact with man, they can create new fields which over long periods, have negative effects on the ion and electron exchanges of the body cells. Eventually these long-term and repeated changes produce confusion and disorder in the cells.

•Polarity Pollution Caused by Electrical Currents

Electrical wires and cables, electrical appliances, and generally

anywhere that electricity exists, a field will be created to which we are exposed. These fields can cause a disturbance in the cellular fields, causing cellular dysfunction which leads to human illness.

A.2.Wave Pollution

This form of pollution stems from the wide use of different wavelengths produced by telecommunications. Today's world, in a sense, is a world of man-made waves. We are constantly bombarded by millions of waves with various frequencies such as radio, television, wireless, cell phones, and so on, which all pass through our bodies. These waves, with a high probability, produce negative effects and disturbances on the human body. Traversing of different waves in turn may create their own new fields, leading to cellular disturbance.

A.3.Conductivity Pollution

This is caused by the existence of synthetic insulators and artificial products that inhibit or limit the ion and electron exchange between the human body and the ground, such as shoes with plastic soles and socks with synthetic fibers. As illustrated in Figure 23, human beings are affected, through the air, by field currents and magnetic waves, and by electric and ion exchanges through the ground. This exposure causes the absorption of free electrons/ions that are discharged through our feet and other limbs that touch the ground. Clothes with synthetic fibers reduce the level of free electron and ion absorption, and this can create problems and endanger human beings' health. As human beings become increasingly detached from their natural physiological conditions, the connection between the human body and the Earth is disrupted. This disruption inhibits the free exchange of electrons and ions, and disturbs the natural electrical charge of the cells.

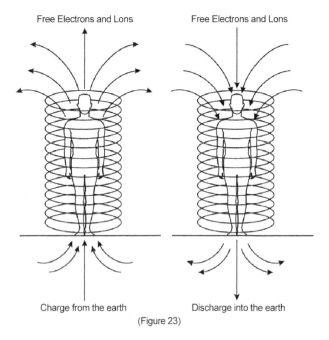

Free Electrons and Lons   Free Electrons and Lons

Charge from the earth   Discharge into the earth

(Figure 23)

The lifestyle, career, and man-made utilities all contribute to this ever-increasing detachment. For example, in occupations such as aviation that involves spending hours in flights, pilots are exposed only to the aerial magnetic conditions and have no connection to the Earth to secure their electron balance. Therefore, after hours of flying they might feel more fatigued than a person working on land. Another example is people who spend long hours working inside a submarine or perhaps people who in the future will be living/working inside space stations. They will face some inadequacies in conductivity and need to devise a strategy to overcome this obstacle.

A bare-footed connection with the Earth will electrically charge the body like a reservoir (through ion and electron exchanges), which can in turn have positive effect on the cells' functioning.

One branch of non-conventional therapy involves the method wherein the therapist directly comes into contact with the Earth and nature, and becomes charged like a reservoir. After coming into contact with the patient, he unloads his charge on to (discharge into) the patient. As a result, the therapist's discharge, charges the patient, thereby improves the patient's general condition. But the charging of the patient, results in a discharge of the therapist who becomes greatly exhausted and requires another recharge after every treatment. With this method, the types of treatable illnesses are very limited and include primarily illnesses stemming from inadequacies of ion and electron exchange in the cells. However this is not effective in treating physical deficiencies such as spinal distortions, congenital disorders, and so on.

Important Note: This method has no application in Faradarmani.

B) Effect of Celestial Bodies

Just like the Earth, all celestial bodies possess a magnetic field that affects all of us, such as when the Moon and the Sun are in specific positions and times, like the position of the "Moon in the Scorpio," which is when the Moon is aligned with the constellation Scorpio. Historical evidence has shown that the level of physical, psychological, and mental disorders peak during this celestial alignment. Infact,human beings are constantly under the influence of magnetic fields and other celestial fields.

Figure 24 shows the changes in the polarity fields of the Sun and the Earth which is a result of their influences on one-another. In particular times these changes are more intense and have stronger results on humans.

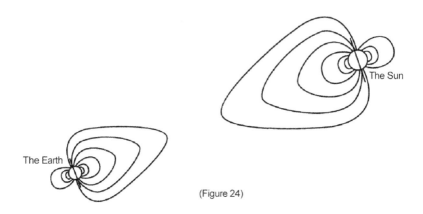

(Figure 24)

Natural Treatment and Human Energy Fields

Nature is man's best healer. Indeed, man's illnesses essentially stem from his gradual detachment from nature through the centuries. Spending time in nature, far from technology, is one of the best resources for man to overcome deficiencies in his different energy fields. Man, while spending time outdoors, has experienced the healing power of nature, and considers it as the effect of clean air and oxygen, the positive effects of which are irrefutable. However in fact, the major factor is exposure to natural fields that help to correct human beings' energy fields, which in turn leads to general health improvements.

As mentioned before, the condition for making use of the gifts of nature is keeping distant from modern life style as much as possible and being at peace with nature. So whenever we spend time in nature, we must distance ourselves from metals and allow the soles of our feet to come into contact with the Earth as much as we can to make the most out of the endless beneficial effects of nature.

Faradarmani and Organ Transplant

Sometimes an organ transplant is rejected despite all the necessary precautions and various testing that assures the success of the transplanted organ, however without any apparent problem, the organ is rejected, and attacked by the body's immune system. According to *Faradarmani* the reason for such a **rejection is the disharmony and incompatibility of cellular intelligence (consciousness)** between the transplanted organ and the recipient's body.

This prevents the body's management system (*Zehn*, Mind or Mental body or the manager of cellular consciousness) from identifying the new organ, and therefore it is attacked by the immune system. Even in cases where the transplanted part is taken from the patient's body himself, there is still a possibility of incompatibility in the cellular consciousness. For example, in an open-heart surgery, the transplanted artery which is taken from the patient's leg may be rejected. In such cases, the person had most probably endured an intense amount of consciousness conflict in his body (prior to surgery). Factors such as distress which impairs body management can create consciousness disorder in the body, and lead to incompatibility in cellular consciousness, and organ rejection.

Blood transfusion can also have unpleasant side effects on the patient's body, psyche, and Zehn. After a blood transfusion, for complete conformity and natural integrity in cellular consciousness time is required.

The Principle of "Survival of the Fittest" from the Perspective of Cellular Consciousness

Being contaminated with micro-organisms does not necessarily cause illness; as many people are indeed carriers of micro-organisms but do not become ill themselves. For example, some people carry the HIV virus but do not show any symptoms of AIDS. Similarly, some carriers of the tuberculosis or influenza viruses are not affected by the disease themselves.

Major epidemics have broken out throughout history, and contagious diseases have taken heavy tolls on life in human societies. However, there have always been a number of people who did not catch the disease and have survived these catastrophes. Taking into consideration that these people have undeniably been contaminated like the rest of the people who were under the same condition, how can we explain their survival?

From the viewpoint of *Faradarmani* we must say that those who stayed alive had a healthy cellular consciousness management. Nature had chosen them according to the principle of survival of the fittest in regards to their cellular consciousness. The body's immune system of this group, because of being equipped with a healthy cellular consciousness, could defend itself from the attack of micro-organisms. As a result, in spite of the inevitable environmental contamination, the individual does not become ill[17].

Important Principles in Faradarmani

Certain principles in *Faradarmani* pave the path and provide further clarification of the treatment process.

> •**Principle:** The first priority in treatment is with common conventional medicine, and when this has proved ineffective, the patien can request assistance from a Fara-therapist for experiencing Faradarmani. This principle must be explained to the patient.

In this respect a Fara-therapist is someone who follows up the effects of *Faradarmani* on the patient (*Faradarmani* receiver)[18]. A Faradarmani receiver is usually someone who has tried conventional methods of treatment however has not gained the desired results. It can be assumed that anyone wishing to try Faradarmani, has not achieved results from conventional medicine.

17- Each and every particle in the universe is influenced by a variety of fields such as gravitational, electromagnetic, whereas in Faradarmani another field is introduced named "The Consciousness Field". The overall behavior of particles in the consciousness field varies from their behavior in other fields. For more details on consciousness immunity and its effect on environmental contamination please refer to the book "Faradarmani", M.A. Taheri)

18- In fact upon applying Faradarmani, the Fara-therapist, by connecting (Ettesal) the patient to the Interuniversal Consciousness, exposes him to Interuniversal Consciousness for treatment to take place.

•**Principle:** Those who are on medication-despite not having gained the desired results from conventional treatments- and who cannot suddenly discontinue their medication, can use *Faradarmani* and follow up the treatment progress under the supervision of their medical doctor. Such patients can decrease the dosage of their medication under their doctors' recommendation. It is obvious that in such cases,all the responsibility of changes in medication lies on the patient.

•**Principle:** [For the Fara-therapist] being informed of the patient's type of illness has no effect in *Faradarmani* results. In some cases the illness of an individual is a confidential issue and the Fara-therapist has no right to ask questions on this matter, unless of course the pa tient, himself, is willing to elaborate on his illness. Nevertheless, this information does not help the Fara-therapist.

•**Principle:** When the Fara-therapist establishes a link for an individual, he himself will also be exposed to *Ettesal* and will in turn be scanned by the Interuniversal Consciousness.

•**Principle:** [In summary Faradarmani's treatment procedure is as follows:]

Faradarmani → Interuniversal Consciousness's Scanning process → Externalization → Treatment

•**Principle:** Inability to feel the Scanning process and the *Ettesal* can be related to the following issues:

-Muddled Mind (Disturbed Mind, extreme chaos of the Mind (Zehn)

-Depression

-Mental Lock: A mental lock is the practical result of programming the subconscious mind during infancy and childhood. In the majority of people this programming is based on logic, science, and knowledge. [In adulthood] this program prevents the entry and perception of subjects which are considered non-logical [by this part of subconscious mind]. It censors any information outside its logical framework, and thus prevents the individual from accepting and experiencing metaphysical phenomena or any related experience and feelings. In fact, this software is programmed in a way not to accept anything outside of logic, science, and what is assumed as reality.

Since *Faradarmani* treatment cannot be scientifically and rationally justified, the subconscious program will not allow the entry of information related to this matter, and will create a **mental lock**; breaking this lock may take some time.

Other possible reasons for this phenomenon can be:

-Lack of presence in *Faradarmani's Halqeh* [not being an impartial observer], being biased and having negative preconceptions, making a mockery of this matter, and so on.

Note: Except for the last issue [lack of presence, being biased and so on], not feeling the Scanning or *Ettesal* by the Fara-therapist or *Faradarmani* receiver has no effect on the *Faradarmani* treatment.

Note: *Faradarmani* is not Energy Therapy. Energy Therapy relies on the polarity field of the therapist -all human beings have a polarity field that may be stronger in some people- whereas *Faradarmani* is dependent on the Interuniversal Consciousness. Energy Therapy is a very minor subcategory of Faradarmani, and it is necessary for the Fara-therapist to understand this to be able to introduce the *Interuniversal Consciousness* in the best way possible[19].

> •**Principle:** A number of Fara-therapists can simultaneously apply *Faradarmani* on one patient, and a number of patients can simultaneously receive *Faradarmani* from one Fara-therapist; either way, **the end results are the same.** Since the *Interuniversal Consciousness* carries out the treatment, there is no difference between Fara-therapists.

> •**Principle:** Becoming present in the *Halqeh* of Unity does not require any faith or belief, and the only required condition is being an impartial observer.

> •**Principle:** The process of *Faradarmani* treatment is independent of the type of illness, including congenital or genetic, organ dysfunction, infectious diseases, mechanical defects, old age and exhaustion, mental,

---

19- In Faradarmani, once a link (Ettesal) is established through the Interuniversal Consciousness, with the correction of the ion and electron exchanges in the cells, the polarity field is automatically corrected and it expands. Therefore, there is no need for correction through any hand movements.

psychological, psychosomatic and mentosomatic (mind-body) disorders, chronic or acute, and the duration of illness.

•**Principle:** In long-distance *Ettesal* there is no limitation to the number of times a patient can undertake Faradarmani, and the patient can use this ser vice as often as he wishes anytime during the 24 hours, day or night. Patients, who are in a different time zone than their Fara-therapist, can an nounce the preferred time for a *Faradarmani* session **according to their own local time** to the Fara-therapist, and the Fara-therapist will then announce this time [the patient's local time] to the Inte runiversal Consciousness, and there is no need to convert this into Fara-therapist's local time.

•**Principle:** Long and short-distance *Faradarmani* are the same in essence and the same results are achieved through both types of treatment. The Fara-therapist's merits, talents, or capabilities, and so on do not affect the results.

•**Principle:** In *Faradarmani* there is no need to ask permission or acquire a report from the below listed types of patients, however it is necessary for at least one of the patient's companions (family, friends, and so on) to be informed that *Faradarmani* is being carried out and be aware of the course of treatment.

-Infants and children

-Patients in coma

-Very elderly patients

-Mentally retarded patients

-Psychological or mental patients

-Emergency cases

-Special illnesses such as Alzheimer's disease in which the patient is not able to report.

•**Principle:** In order to avoid any possible misunderstanding and misconception, it is better to apply Faradarmani, as much as possible, from long-distance and without touch of the hand. In addition the Fara-therapist must avoid feeding anything (even water) to the patient during the session. If necessary, this should be done only by those accompanying the patient to prevent any possible doubtsof attributing the treatment to anyone or anything other than the Interuniversal Consciousness.

•**Principle:** Practicing *Faradarmani* does not bring any negative karma or consequences for the individual, because it is only performed throughthe Divine Consciousness and it is not the Fara-therapist who carries out the treatment.

•**Principle: Faradarmani must not be practiced if the Fara-therapist has not yet received the protective layer (Shield). This is because the Fara-therapist would be exposed to the patient's negative emissions and also to the infiltration of Non-organic beings, which both have short and long term negative effects on the Fara-therapist.**

The protective layer is entrusted to the Fara-therapist after completing the written text of oath, pledging to make positive and humanitarian use of Faradarmani. Upon receiving this layer, the Fara-therapist is then protected against the emissions of defective cellular consciousness, other negative emissions, and infiltration by Non-organic beings. It also puts the patient in a confident protection during *Faradarmani* (in both long or short-distance Faradarmani).

•**Principle:** As it is the *Interuniversal Consciousness* who actually carries out Faradarmani, the Fara-therapist does not have the right to consider any kind of disease as incurable.

•**Principle:** Both long and short-distance *Faradarmani* treatments are possible for the reason that *Interuniversal Consciousness* is the collection of the consciousness governing the universe, it is neither energy nor matter; and is independent of dimensions of time and space.

•**Principle:**As it is the *Interuniversal Consciousness* who actually carries out Faradarmani, the Fara-therapist does not have the right to consider any kind of disease as incurable or attribute anything (power of healing) to himself.

•**Principle:** Considering that Divine Consciousness requires no supplement, nothing can be added to it under any name or label. This can be proved easily; because by omitting and disregarding such insertions, it will be clearly observed that the *Halqeh* of Unity still works and this disgraces the deceivers and those who try to make alterations in the original concept. Therefore, in this regard there is absolutely no room for any personal alteration, and this would be only a sign of the individual's desire to show off and brag and proclaim himself boastfully.

•**Principle:** The long-distance *Ettesal* (link) is effective regardless of patient's physical position; including any posture and manner that is convenient for him such as standing still or moving, sitting down, standing up, lying down, or any convenient direction and location; any fixed or mobile place (for example, in a bus, airplane, or ship).

•**Principle:** , illnesses, and the patient's previous record of past illnesses that have either not been treated or only partially treated, are once more reviewed [by the Interuniversal Consciousness], and their symptoms are revealed and the process of treatment is initiated according to the below displayed graphs.

In some cases, treatment is quick and follows the trend illustrated below:

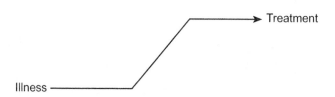

In many cases, after the symptoms of pain and illness reach their peak, they start to decrease until the complete treatment is achieved. The "peak of illness" means that the illness's symptoms are reconstructed based on the cellular memory. Upon this display these symptoms are treated accordingly, and are in turn replaced by healthy cellular consciousness. For instance, if a lump exists in the patient's body, *Faradarmani* scanning will identify the lump and indications revealing the lump's existence will be manifested, however in no way will the lump grow bigger. Instead, only the symptoms and pains of the lump will appear, that is followed by the treatment process and healing.

Another example is a patient suffering from an allergy: after receiving *Faradarmani Ettesal*, the allergy symptoms may begin to intensify, and during the externalization process, it may reach its peak, and thereafter decrease, and the illness is treated accordingly. In a patient with migraine attacks, the typical symptoms of the migraine often reach a peak and afterwards with the decrease of the symptoms, improvement and healing will manifest itself.

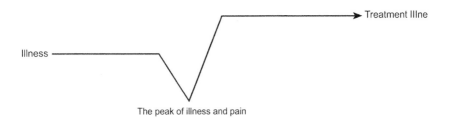

Treatment Illne

Illness

The peak of illness and pain

Treatment of psychosomatic patients occurs according to the following graphs:

1.Diagram P-A: Psychosomatic Patients

Treatment

Illness

2.Diagram P-B: Psychosomatic Patients

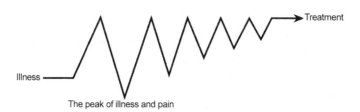

The peak of illness and pain

2.Diagram P-C: Psychosomatic Patients which their problems Lies in their worldview

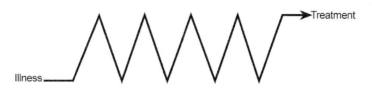

Treatment of patients with mental disorders is as follows.

1. Diagram M-A1

2. Diagram M-A2

3. Diagram M-B1

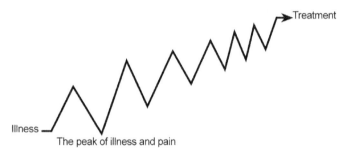

4. Diagram M-B2

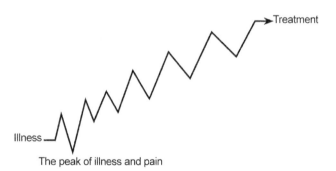

5. Diagram M-CA1: with the general trend of Diagram M-A1
(But with an irregular pattern)

6. Diagram M-CA2: with the general trend of Diagram M-A2
(But with an irregular pattern)

7. Diagram M-CB1: with the general trend of Diagram M-B1
(But with an irregular pattern)

8. Diagram M-CB2: with the general trend of Diagram M-B2
(But with an irregular pattern)

Treatment of Patients with Psychological (Emotional) and Physical (Somatic) Illness Is According to the Following Graphs:

A. Without Externalization

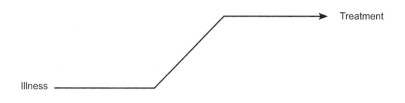

B. With Discharge

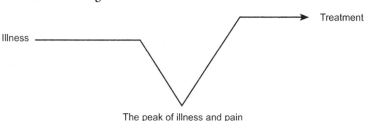

A *Faradarmani* scan also includes externalization of childhood fears that have been recorded inside the subconscious of a patient's mind. In this case, we will be faced with two types of reports. The first type are the patients who did not have a history and report of previous fears or phobias, but after a *Faradarmani* scan, they encounter vague and unknown fears about which they have no information. In most cases, these fears arise at the beginning, and after one episode of externalization they will diminish and be treated. This externalization may come in the form of a nightmare during sleep.

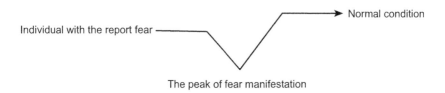

The second type is the patients who have a history and report of fear, as a part of their present complaints. In this case, the fear might increase at the beginning of the scanning process but later decrease and finally disappear.

• **Principle:** Once an individual is connected to the positive network and exposed to its awareness, the negative network also attempts to establish a link, and consequently tries to open a window towards negative awareness for the individual;offering powers such as mind- reading, to exert influence or gain power over somebody by using magic (charm), future telling,and so on.

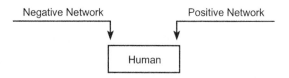

The influence of the positive and negative networks, and receiving awareness from any of these networks could occur during sleep or while awake (see Positive and Negative Networks, Chapter Four). It is imperative to avoid accepting awareness from the negative network.

•**Principle:** In Interuniversal Mysticism (*Erfan-e Halqeh*), human interventions, personal characteristics, geographic and regional conditions, personal abilities and facilities, and so on, have no role in establishing a link and receiving divine spiritual awareness. Therefore, the below points have no effects on benefiting from the *Halqeh*es of Interuniversal Mysticism and on individual's *Kamal*-acceptability:

-Age, gender, race or nationality, talent, level of education, aknowledge, mentality and ideology, beliefs, and so on.

-Abstinence, exercise, nutrition, and so on.

-Morphology or temperament types: according to
Damavi(*Sanguine*), Balghami (*Phelgmatic*), Sodaie (*Atrabilious*) and Safravi (*Bilious*) types; or Vata, Pita and Kafa, or endomorphic, mesomorphic, ectomorphic features, and so on.

-The facial features of people based on physiognomy.

-Endeavour, struggle, will power and so on.

-Imagination and visualization, chants and mantras, drawing symbols and signs, inculcation and repetition, concentration, and so on.

-Numerology, astrology, the position of the stars, the individual's date of birth, and so on.

Therefore every human being in any corner of the world, regardless of all the above-mentioned features, has the potential for inner transformation and *Kamal*-seeking.

•**Principle:** Applying *Faradarmani* on others, in turn, helps the Fara-therapist's illnesses to be treated.

•**Principle:** *Faradarmani* can also be applied on animals and plants, and is effective on them.

Important Recommendation: Let us not forget to express our gratitude to God after receiving any kind of benefit from the Interuniversal Consciousness.

Knowing the following points helps the *Faradarmani* receiver:

•Being in the state of total surrendering and an impartial observer at all matters, and avoiding any kind of imagination, visualization, chanting and mantras, self-hypnosis, drawing symbols and signs, and so on.

•Understanding the nature of the Scanning process, during the symptoms of previous illnesses is brought up to the surface (externalization). At this stage the patient might initially seem to be in a bad condition due to severe externalization. Of course, the patient must realize that it is only the symptoms of the illness that have temporarily increased and not the illness itself; thus, it has absolutely no threat for the patient [an increase in manifested symptoms is happening while the illness itself is being cured].

•Having sufficient information on the important principles of *Faradarmani*.

•Being familiar with the graphs and different trends of the treatment process, the Scanning stage, and the externalization of different illnesses.

A Definition of Depression (According to *Faradarmani*)

An individual's interpretation of his surroundings, the material world, and external events are reported to his brain via his sensors (senses) and then passes through a filter and framework which we call **Perceptual or world-viewing Filter**. This filter is programmed in advance based on the type of thinking, experiences, personal understandings, and environmental effects; then, it accordingly evaluates the intensity and weakness of the current events, their existential values, and other criteria.

Perceptual or world-viewing Filter in the broad sense can be defined as the individual's interpretation of himself and the universe. The Zehn's perceptual reaction to an event is manifested only after the event passes through the filter of perception, and then, according to the programs inside this framework, our conception of that event is finally formed.

The Zehn's perceptual reaction is then followed by the reaction of the psyche, which determines the type of our emotional response to the event. After this stage, the deduction of the Zehn and psyche is transmitted to the brain in the form of messages that are translated by the brain into the language of the physical body, which this time is in the form of chemical and neural messages. These messages are then relayed to the body where the proper reactions will take place. In brief, our perceptions and emotions after being transmitted and translated, are revealed to us in the form of chemical messages by different parts of the brain.

The schematic chart below displays the different stages of depression according to *Faradarmani*.

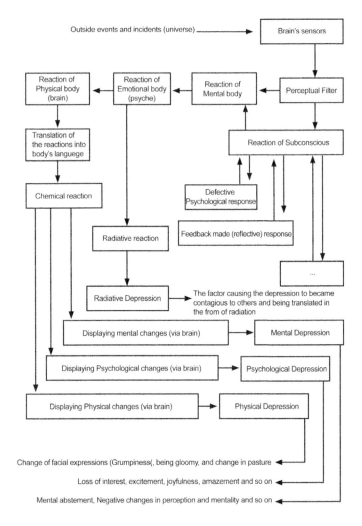

According to the schematic chart above, emissive (emission-based) depression is the initial stage in which the individual's vibes (emissions)[20] start to change (see next page). At this stage, the individual shows no other apparent sign of depression and does not express anything regarding depression himself. However after a while,

---

20- "Consciousness" possesses "emission or vibes." The consciousness effect is conveyed via emission or vibe. People in the vicinity of one another are affected by each other's consciousness emission. Consciousness emission is neither frequency nor particle in nature; it lacks chemical or physical effects, and only produces a consciousness effect. Human being's thoughts, feelings, and illnesses (cellular emission) also possess consciousness emission.

depression infects the Zehn and what is called mental depression initiates; thus, the signs of depression gradually begin to reflect in the individual's perceptions. At this stage, depression has not yet affected the emotions of the individual, and he can still express positive emotions. As time passes and this trend continues, the psyche is affected and the emotions are consequently influenced by depression in the form of tendency toward negative feelings, which we call psychological depression. Now, the individual's vibes are completely negative, and he has messed-up perceptions and negative emotions.

Therefore, following this trend, the destructive effects of depression are transmitted to and seen in the individual's body, his movements, walking, facial expressions, and posture that appears sluggish and out of shape. As the depression continues, the depression vibes (Figure 25) are intensified and completely envelope the entire body. With the passage of time and involvement of the body, eventually the entire body will be taken over by emissive depression through oval shape orbits, preventing the entry of positive currents such as the Vital Force and other universal energies that are crucial for the functioning of the chakras and energy reactors.

Consequently, as a result of such impairment, the psyche loses its ability to differentiate between emotions, and the Zehn loses its ability to distinguish the perceptions. This means that while the individual can still well-understand the meaning of everything, he is not able to perceive the essence and meaning of the events, and he eventually looses his feelings and perceptions towards everything. For example, the individual recognizes his child accurately, but seeing his child does not invoke any feelings in him. As a result, his perception of relations deteriorates, the value and importance of events are lost, and the individual completely loses cognitive contact with his surroundings and reaches the point that we call a **"silent death (imperceptible death)."**

Emissive Depression

When the "software-based world-viewing filter" interprets outside events with a negative outlook, the psycheal body produces negative vibes. This emission is capable of contaminating and affecting other individuals within its vicinity. This means that depression can affect those who come into contact with the depressed individual. As the [Iranian] proverb says, "The disheartened soul disheartens the company." Among those who are at high risk of being contaminated by this negative emission are psychiatrists.

In summary, our thoughts have either a negative or a positive aspect. Positive thoughts produce positive emission that is followed by a positive and flourished spirit.

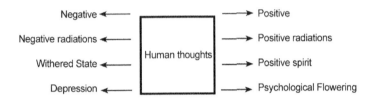

If the individual's emissions are negative, it can contaminate the psycheal body and the emissions [of depression] expand in the shape of oval orbits that seem to emanate from the center of the brain, and can eventually take over the individual's entire existence (Figure 25).

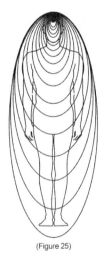

(Figure 25)

The distribution of negative emissions of depression throughout the psycheal body and its superimposition on the physical body

Mental Depression

This is the second stage of depression (after emissive contamination) that engages the individual's Zehn; thus, the influences of negative thoughts will gradually appear in the individual. However in this stage, the individual is still capable of expressing positive emotions such as laughter and humor.

Psychological Depression

The third stage in depression is called "psychological depression," in which the engagement of depression expands from the Mind into the psyche. Thus, the individual's emotions tend to be negative, and in this stage signs of a disheartened and withered spirit can be observed in the individual.

Physical Depression

Finally, this condition finds its way into the physical body of the individual, where the signs of depression can be observed through changes in his facial expression, the speech and movements also take on a certain shape, followed by the blockage of entrance of positive emissions including the Interuniversal Consciousness.

Ultimately, once the whole being of the individual is completely enveloped by depressive emission, he will reach a condition which is called the stage of **silent death (imperceptible death)**." In this stage, the individual will lose all his cognitive communication with the outside world and everything will lose its meaning, and even if he understands the meaning of things, what he sees or hears will not create any motivation in him.

Therefore, among those who initially do not properly feel the Interuniversal Consciousness's *Ettesal*, are the depressed people who might not feel the scanning process and its flow at all, or might feel the scanning flow only up to a certain point in their body. In this way we can examine the extent of the psycheal body that is affected by the negative energy of depression.

Testing the Existence of Emissive Depression via the Vital Force Scan

Upon applying the Vital Force scanning on an individual, we realize that when the Vital Force moves through the body, it penetrates up to a certain area where it is stopped and locked. The individual reports feeling a kind of force that blocks the movement of the flow. This gives us an estimation of the area in the body which is under the influence of negative emission of depression. By continuing the treatment process (continuous Scanning), the Vital Force gradually makes its way toward the center of the brain (Figure 25), and the negative energy of depression will be neutralized and depression will be treated.

Faradarmani Graphs and Reasons for Relapse of Illness

A considerable percentage of patients are cured and survive the illness with just one session of Faradarmani, regardless of their type of illness, whether being chronic or acute, or how long they have been suffering from the illness.

The course of recovery of such patients is illustrated in the following graph:

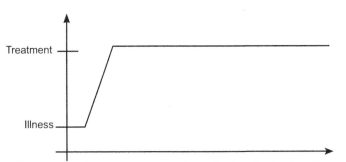

The diagram of treatment process for patients with physical illnesses

However, in some cases, after the patient is fully treated and recovered, he will have relapse of illness. The reasons for such relapse can be summarized as follows:

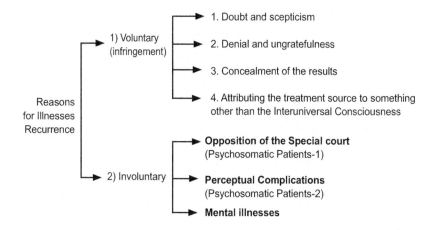

Reasons for Relapse of Illnesses (Willingly)

This type of relapse happens when the patient makes a voluntary infringement (violation of *Faradarmani* principles) by somehow ignoring or denying the role of the *Interuniversal Consciousness* in the treatment of his illness. Some examples of this violation include: doubt and skepticism [after being treated], denial and ungratefulness, concealing the [positive] gained results, and attributing the source of treatment to somewhere other than the Interuniversal Consciousness.

Therefore, in case of such violations, it is possible that after the time (T1) in which the patient's condition has improved, the process reverses suddenly and the patient's condition returns to its initial state, as before the treatment.

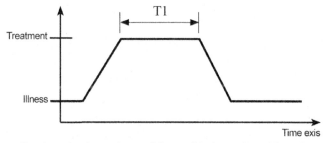

The chart of patients who are violators of the Interuniversal Consciousness

Reasons for Relapse of Illnesses (Unwillingly)

This type of relapse occurs when psychological or mental problems are the primary and main cause of the illness, or in cases where the patient suffers from problems in their worldview (viewpoint-based illnesses). In such cases, the patient plays no role in the relapse of the illness, however based on certain mechanisms of the Zehn(Mind) and psyche, their treatment encounters resistance (The High Court's resistance, page 229),and thus the illness recurs. Nevertheless this resistance can be overcome, and the patient can eventually be relieved from his illness by persistently following up and continuing *Faradarmani* treatment.

The graphs below show the treatment course for each category of patients with unwilling reasons for relapse, which are examined closer in the following sections.

A. Resistance of the High Court

A.1. Diagram P-A: Psychosomatic Patients

The condition of this group of patients initially improves, but after the T1 time span, they experience a relapse [due to the resistance of the High Court, page ..]; however, they report that their general condition has improved in comparison to their initial state. As the *Faradarmani* course of treatment is followed, the patient again resumes his favorable condition during the T2 interval; the duration of T2 is longer than T1. This state continues until the illness relapses again, however this time the patient's general condition is reported even better compared to the previous relapse. This progress continues until the patient's condition is stabilized at a satisfactory level[21].

21- On the view that Faradarmani focuses on a deeply-rooted treatment of illnesses and not only the relief of symptoms, in psychosomatic patients, in line with the gradual resolution of High Court problems –with the aid of the Interuniversal Consciousness- the patients' general condition also improves.

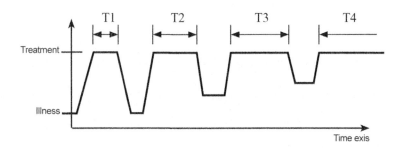

Diagram P-A: The Course of Recovery during Treatment of Psychosomatic Patients, High Court

A.2. Diagram P-B: Psychosomatic Patients

The diagram for these patients is similar to diagram A, with the difference that the first relapse of the illness which happens after the time interval of T1, is noticeably worse than the patient's initial state. In a way that it might cause the patient to panic and discontinue the course of treatment. Nevertheless, continuing the fluctuating process of treatment will eventually return the patient to his satisfactory condition.

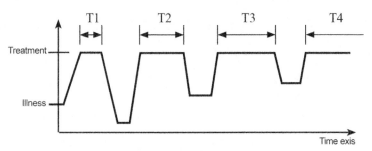

Diagram P-B: The Course of Recovery during Treatment of Psychosomatic Patients, High Court

B. Mentosomatic Illnesses or Viewpoint-Rooted (Worldview) Illnesses

The illness of some individuals is caused by problems and weaknesses in their worldview and way of thinking. For example, if the starting point of an illness is the patient's phobia of death, after being completely treated with Faradarmani, if his viewpoint-rooted problem has not been rectified, the illness might relapse by hearing about the death of someone, seeing a funeral procession, or anything that might remind them of death and dying,

In *Faradarmani* this type of illnesses which stems from the patient's worldview and viewpoint-rooted problems; is called "Mentosomatic Illnesses".

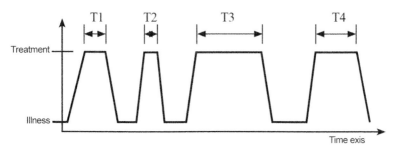

The Diagram of the Course of Recovery during Treatment of Patients with Mentosomatic Problems (High Court)

Therefore, the events that happen just before the relapse of the illness, share a common clue that can help identify the patient's faulty way of thinking.

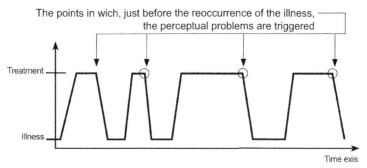

The Diagram of the Course of Recovery during Treatment of Patients with Mentosomatic Problems (High Court)

After the patient understands and accepts that his problem (Mentosomatic illness) stems from his worldview or way of thinking, and he attempts to overcome that, he will be supported by the *Interuniversal Consciousness* and the treatment will reach a stable stage. In such cases, the Fara-therapist must guide the patient and explain the process and mechanism of the related graph for him.

C. Patients with Mental Disorders

According to the classification of Faradarmani, one type of illness is mental disorders. In such cases, the perceptions of these patients are considered as abnormal compared to others, for example, obsession (Obsessive Compulsive Disorder), schizophrenia (hallucinations), paranoia, sexual perversion, absentmindedness, hyperactivity, phobias (irrational and excessive fears), and so on.

In *Faradarmani* there is a specific approach to this type of patients, and the treatment for such cases lies within a special branch of treatment called **"Defensive Emission"**, which is thoroughly discussed in the book written by the present author titled **Non-organic Beings.**

The following charts show the course of recovery during treatment of mental disorders. As you see, the process of treatment follows a positive gradient which is called **the treatment line.** The progress through this line generally follows a fluctuating zigzag pattern that is displayed below in the general **groups A and B.**

C.a) Group A Graphs

The patients in this group progress along the treatment line in a fluctuating zigzag manner, and in each relapse, their condition is better than the previous time. In type A1, as the patient progresses along the treatment line, the teeth of the zigzags become bigger and the duration of each tooth increases and prolongs. In contrast, for patients corresponding to type A2, as one goes along the treatment line, the teeth get smaller and their durations shorten.

Graph M-A1: Mental Disorders

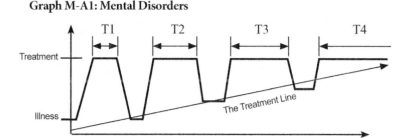

Diagram M-A1: Treatment of Patients with Mental Complications

Graph M-A2: Mental Disorders

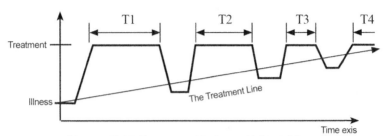

Diagram M-A2: Treatment of Patients with Mental Complications

Diagram M-A3: Similar to Diagram M-A1 (but with an irregular pattern)

Diagram M-A4: Similar to Diagram M-A2 (but with an irregular pattern)

C.b) Group B Graphs

The treatment graph for this group of patients is similar to the above mentioned graphs and follows the sloped treatment line, with the difference that at the first zigzag tooth, the relapse is worse than the patient's initial state. Therefore, after the first reoccurrence, the patient reports a worsening of his condition. However, by continuing *Faradarmani* treatment, their condition improves in accordance to the treatment line. This group generally has two types of graphs:

Graph M-B1: Mental Disorders

On this graph, the teeth of the zigzags become larger and the intervals between the relapses increase.

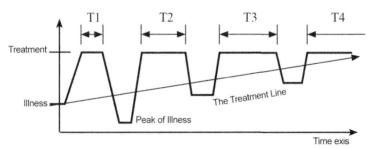

Diagram M-B1: Treatment of Patients with Mental Complications

Graph M-B2: Mental Disorders

In this case, the teeth get smaller and the intervals between relapses decrease. These graphs are not particularly desirable conditions, because after experiencing the first relapse that worsens the patient's condition, the patient might become worried and decide not to continue the treatment. In this case, it is the Fara-therapist's duty to inform the patient and explain the graph which greatly helps the patient to understand the process.

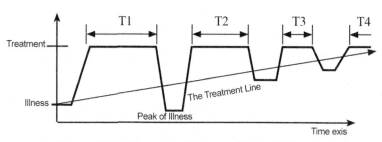

Diagram M-B1: Treatment of Patients with Mental Complications

Graph M-B3: Similar to Diagram M-B1 but with irregular pattern

Graph M-B4: Similar to Diagram M-B2 but with irregular pattern

D. Patients with Psychological or Emotional Disorders

The pattern of treatment in patients with psychological disorders generally has no relapse and initiates immediately. It progresses along the sloped treatment line; the only difference lies in the timeframe in different patients for the satisfactory condition to be stabilized.

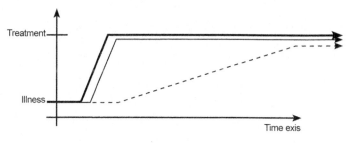

Treatment of Patients with "psychological" conditions

The Treatment Graph for Patients with Multiple Disorders (Mixed Graph)

An individual can suffer from multiple disorders including more than one of the above-mentioned categories. Therefore, after a *Faradarmani* scan, the multiple disorders are all revealed at the same time and their externalization starts. As the treatment of each disease follows its own special graph, patient's reports usually sound abnormal or nonsensical.

In reality, the treatment charts of several different illnesses have been overlapped, creating an unusual pattern in the patient's condition. Due to the simultaneous externalization of all the symptoms, if the patient is not informed and convinced, he might get confused and decide to discontinue the treatment.

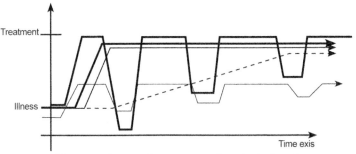

Treatment diagram for patients with multiple disorders

Definition of Mental Disorders

•Any abnormal thought, behavior, tendency, and factor that disturbs human perceptions (i.e., sexual perversion, sadism, masochism, restlessness, and bad temper without a reason)

•Various hallucinations (visual, auditory, tactile, mental, and so on)

•Obsessive behavior (OCD)

•Bipolar disorder

•Multiple personality

•Phobia or illogical fears

•Suicidal tendencies

Definition of Psychological or Emotional Disorders

Any chronic and permanent psychological or emotional abnormality that has become a part of an individual's existence or any factor that causes abnormal emotional tendencies such as:

- Constant discontent with oneself, others, and the environment
- Not being able to tolerate the condition of one's surroundings and constant vulnerability
- Anxiety, stress, and worry
- Feelings of guilt or having guilt complex
- Melancholy
- Lack of motivation; aimlessness and apathy
- Feeling depressed

It is worth noting that most psychological problems stem from the Zehn and are in fact considered as mental problems. Although feelings such as worry, stress, and anxiety are parts of our emotions and classified as psychological disorders, they actually stem from our mental attitude and false worldviews, which in turn infect the psyche. Similarly a guilty conscience and dissatisfaction derive from a faulty Zehn which has been programmed falsely. As a result Zehn produces false conceptions of the world and our surroundings, and by creating irrational and totally unrealistic fears it imposes this fear on the psyche.

Definition of Illness According to Interuniversalism

According to Interuniversalism illness is defined as any kind of defect in any of the infinite constituents of the human existence. In other words different bodies of man (physical, psycheal, mental, astral, and so on) must be in contact and harmony with each other (equilibrium-phase of bodies); the different chakras must be functioning properly without any defect or obstruction; the fourteen channels of energy (which are considered in acupuncture) must be in balance; the surrounding energy fields (polarity and bio-plasma fields) must be in order and in a good state; healthy cellular consciousness and molecular and cellular frequency should not deviate from their original state; and so on.

However, according to Interuniversalism, there is another method for classifying illnesses. Man's existence, like other constituents of the universe, is composed of three major elements: Awareness (Consciousness, Intelligence), Matter, and Energy (As mentioned before, Matter and Energy are created by Awareness). Accordingly, an illness can be caused in any of these three elements as the result of changes and transformations that take place within an individual's existence. Human existence functions in a uniformed way; therefore, illness [in any of the three elements] will spread into the other parts. Thus, it can be said:

Illness in Matter includes mechanical injuries, toxic effects, wear and tear, fatigue and aging.

Illness in Energy includes an imbalance in energy channels, chakras, polarity fields, and so on.

Illness in Awareness includes disorder in cellular consciousness, such as cancer, and so on.

Definition of Hysteria

Man consists of different bodies including the physical body, mental body, psycheal body, and astral body and so on. A disruption in the equilibrium (asynchrony) among these bodies can result in the manifestation of a state that begins with a simple confusion and may continue to the brink of hysteria. The following analogy is provided to help in understanding the mechanism of this issue.

Consider a city in which its developmental projects are administered by different organizations such as the City Council, telecommunications, electricity, water and sewage, gas, subway, and so on. A city which does not have an organized system is subject to chaos and confusion. For example, one day the City Council decides to apply fresh asphalt on the streets; after which the water and sewage organization digs a channel in the same street for replacing the sewage system, and after reconstructing the asphalt by the City Council, another organization attempts to implement their own project by digging through the streets. This trend continues in a way that eventually results in chaos including financial damages. This chaos is related to the absence of cooperation and harmony between the different organizations and the absence of a unified management for executing these tasks and establishing a communication line.

The existence of man resembles such a city, and a typical individual has such a disorganized existence with each of the different bodies acting independently; for example, the mental body, psycheal body, and physical body each act independently and have little or no communication with each other, and the individual cannot often remember even the simplest daily life subjects or might even completely lose control and become deranged when confronted with trivial matters.

The ultimate limit of this condition is called **"hysteria,"** which is when the individual loses control while also losing all sense of time and place, and later on he may not even remember anything about the event. Therefore, as a result of the disconnection between the bodies, perceptions [mental body] and emotions [psycheal body] lose their connection with the physical body, and thus the memory of the event becomes inaccessible.

Definition of the Brain in Faradarmani

Brain is the collection of antennae that transmit the information received from the different internal and external senses of the physical body to the different existing bodies (such as mental body; in charge of the perceptions and psycheal body; in charge of the emotions), and also receive information from these bodies and translate them into the language of the physical body.

In the world of science, man's brain is considered as a super computer that commands the body and directs all vital and intellectual activities (thoughts) of human beings. In order to examine the brain more precisely and to determine its related activities, we first consider the way that organizational and vital activities are controlled:

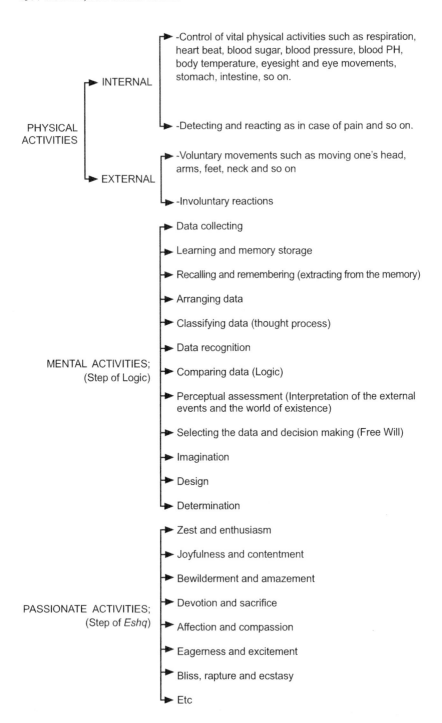

PHYSICAL ACTIVITIES

INTERNAL
- -Control of vital physical activities such as respiration, heart beat, blood sugar, blood pressure, blood PH, body temperature, eyesight and eye movements, stomach, intestine, so on.
- -Detecting and reacting as in case of pain and so on.

EXTERNAL
- -Voluntary movements such as moving one's head, arms, feet, neck and so on
- -Involuntary reactions

MENTAL ACTIVITIES; (Step of Logic)
- Data collecting
- Learning and memory storage
- Recalling and remembering (extracting from the memory)
- Arranging data
- Classifying data (thought process)
- Data recognition
- Comparing data (Logic)
- Perceptual assessment (Interpretation of the external events and the world of existence)
- Selecting the data and decision making (Free Will)
- Imagination
- Design
- Determination

PASSIONATE ACTIVITIES; (Step of Eshq)
- Zest and enthusiasm
- Joyfulness and contentment
- Bewilderment and amazement
- Devotion and sacrifice
- Affection and compassion
- Eagerness and excitement
- Bliss, rapture and ecstasy
- Etc

Now, there are some questions raised here. For example, a computer must be programmed by an operator (programmer), and then the same programs must be again used by the operator (user); thus, without the existence of an operator no system can program itself, and at the same time use its programs. Therefore, if we regard the brain as a super computer, where is the operator? Is the operator a section of the brain or an independent section [outside the brain]?

Let us now consider this matter from a different angle. We know that the brain is made up of neurons, and a neuron is the distributor of the brain's electric system that acts like an electric contactor[22].

In fact, a collection of neurons form an electrical command circuit which controls all the body's automated systems. In a contactor's electrical command circuit, electric current may be switched on or off by opening and closing the contactors. Similarly, in each second the brain receives pulses from different sensors and receptors, which cause the switches (contactors) to be turned on or off [through stimulation of contactors or neurons]; subsequently, physical and mechanical activities automatically follow.

Similarly, in a neuron the electric current enters from one direction. A neuron's synapses act like switches via a chemical reaction called an acetylcholine reaction, which then either lets the current pass through or stops it. In this way, the electric distribution takes place via the neurons. Overall, a neuron serves either as an insulator or a conductor.

There is a basic difference between a neuron and an electric contactor, and that is that the neuron's electric current is composed of voltage and ampere variation adjustments. Each neuron -through the language of these variations- can receive an infinite number of electrical messages and send them to the adjacent neurons. Thus, vital functions continue automatically with the aid of different internal and external body sensors.

Considering the above brief explanation on neurons, we propose a basic question: Where is the neuron's operator? Does a neuron possess a separate brain? In that case, where is its operator located, especially when no brain has yet been identified for the neuron? (Figure 26)

22- A contactor is an electrically controlled switch used for switching an electrical power circuit.

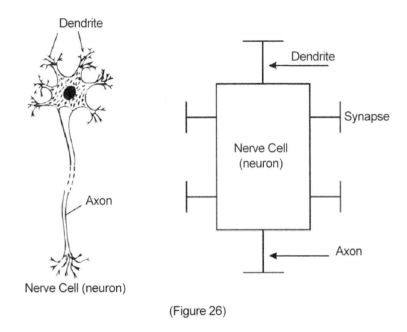

Dendrite

Dendrite

Synapse

Nerve Cell
(neuron)

Axon

Axon

Nerve Cell (neuron)

(Figure 26)

Other questions may be raised about the neuron. Is it, for example, the neuron that decides whether a man should go towards [the world of] unity or multiplicity? What way he should go, this way or that way? Is it the neuron that decides to fall in love and feel intoxicated, amazed, or surprised? Is it the decision of the neuron to devote and sacrifice himself?

It is clear that the neuron, which serves as a mere contactor or switch, is by no means capable of doing this. In fact, some neurons control the automation of the body, and as we will soon see, non-automatic functions get their messages from a center other than the brain. The brain, in fact, reveals the orders it receives from the psycheal and mental bodies and translates them into the language of the physical body.

To further clarify this, we consider several points about the body and the cells.

Managing the Body and the Cells

One of the divisions of the mental body is in charge of managing body and the cells, determining all the cells' duty descriptions. It has a specific anatomy consisting of hundreds of trillions of invisible branches to all cells. Thus, all cells are controlled by this section of the mental body.

The following examples prove this theory.

Example 1: In a known hypnotic experiment, a subject is being inculcated that his forearm is becoming numb and senseless. Upon the suggestion, his forearm becomes perceived as numb. Now, if we poke his palm or upper arm with a needle, he feels the pain, but if we poke a needle into his forearm, he does not feel any pain. Considering the fact that the subject's nervous system works perfectly well, how could it be that his palm and upper arm feel the pain, but his forearm, which is also located on the path of the nervous system, does not feel the pain?

The answer is that by deceiving and misleading the body management system through inculcating an unreal message, the mental body accepts this message and sends an order to the forearm cells to stop reporting the pain (the effect of the inculcation will be studied separately). Therefore, the forearm becomes locally numb. That is to say, the management directs them to do their job by transmitting the cells' duty descriptions.

Example 2: In another hypnotic experiment, a blindfolded man is given the suggestion that a piece of hot iron is about to be put on the palm of his hand, while in reality, it is actually a piece of ice. It is observed that the subject's palm blisters.

Knowing that no hot lump of iron was really involved, then why did the subject's palm blister?

The former answer applies here, too. Once the body management is convinced of this wrong data, it sends the message to the local cells to react against being burnt, and the cells do so. Had the subject's eyes been open to see the ice on his palm, this would never have happened, because the body manager would not be deceived.

Example 3: We now examine a reverse experiment in which the subject is told that he will have a piece of ice on his palm, but in fact a piece of hot iron is placed on his palm. In this case, the body management orders the cells to respond as if ice is placed upon them, and the cells react accordingly. Frostbite symptoms appeared on the subject's palm although hot iron was actually applied.

> **Therefore, we conclude that the body's reaction is a function of the body management and not the actual physical conditions.**

Now that the body management has been deceived by false data, it orders the body to react against ice. It is interesting to ask why the cells were not destroyed when being touched by hot iron? In response, it must be said that a cell's resistance depends on the duty description assigned to it. The cell's resistance is described in each given condition in accordance to that particular condition. For example, marine organisms taken out of 2500 meters depth close to the Italian coast are under an immense amount of pressure and at a temperature of 250° Centigrade, yet their cellular structure is no different from that of other organisms. Should in the future human succeed in bringing other marine organisms living at even lower depths to the surface, it will become evident that their body cells can tolerate very high pressures and temperatures. This proves the point that living organisms can tolerate any environment if their [external] living conditions are defined for that purpose.

The above-mentioned experiment illustrates how some people can walk on fire without burning their feet through long practice and using self-hypnosis methods to enter new commands and change the software of their body management and cell functions. They might even experience frostbite while being on fire. Another example would be people who break the surface ice and go swimming at subzero temperatures.

Example 4: In hysterical illnesses that include paralysis, blindness, and deafness, the organs involved are perfectly healthy, but the patient cannot use these organs. For example, in hysterical blindness, the individual is unable to see. In cases of hysterical paralysis, one is not capable of moving the paralyzed limb.

The same principle applies to hysterical deafness, in which the person involved cannot hear anything. Considering the fact that all these organs are healthy, why can't the person in question control and use them?

The answer is that apart from the mechanism of this kind of disease (which will be considered separately in the following chapter), the body management is somehow convinced to put certain orders into action. For example, to justify exempting a person from certain responsibilities, it transmits messages to a spot on the spinal cord to stop conveying any messages to the upper parts, and so the person becomes paralyzed while being in perfect health and accordingly loses the ability to move, see, or hear.

Example 5: How is it that some people faint upon hearing bad news?

In case of a bad incident, if the Defensive Psychological Response (see page 228) diagnoses an unbearable situation, it sends a message to the body management, and the body management in turn orders the brain to stop conveying any external data until further notice, as a result the person in question faints. Children who experience an acute stomach-ache upon going to school and recover soon after they are assured of staying home, are among similar examples.

All evidence leads to the fact that cells' duty descriptions are assigned from somewhere else. Nevertheless where is the manager of the body? Is it a section of the brain, or is it located elsewhere?

The answer is that this manager is not a section of the brain, and the neurons themselves receive their duty descriptions from this managing section. In fact, the management and control of the hundreds of trillions of cells of which neurons are a part, is somewhere else and will be discussed in the next chapter. The anatomy of this managing section consists of hundreds of trillions of invisible branches which lead to each and every cell and thus transmit their duty descriptions.

Now, knowing this, how does the brain function? To better understand this point, we subdivide the brain's functions as follows:

1. Automation: the section that controls the body functions automatically

2. Control of non-automated reactions.

3.Brain memory.

4. Manifestation of activities related to the Step of Logic and Step of Eshq.

5. Receiving external data [from the environment] through receptors of different senses.

6.Conveying the received messages from the receptors of different senses to the different existing bodies, and also receiving the information that different bodies send.

7.Translating the information received from these bodies into the language of physical body by producing and secreting various chemicals.

Chapter Three

Different Bodies of Man's Existence

Although my heart much sought in this vast land [of creation],

it did not find a thread (it didn't get to know even the tiniest bit),

in spite of much details that it explored.

From my heart rose thousands of suns,

Still could not reach the mystery of the Kamal of a tiny particle.

-Abu Saeed Abil Kheir

The human being consists of thousands of different bodies that constitute the non-physical part of his existence (beyond the visible and tangible frequency range of human). As was briefly discussed in the brain function, many of man's perceptual fields are beyond a cell's capability. For instance, what does a physician mean when stating that a patient's hopeful attitude gives him a better chance of recovery? How can a neuron be in high spirits or cause this hopefulness? Is it possible for a contactor/switch (a neuron) to cause high spirits?

The same applies to when psychology refers to the collective soul. In any case, as mentioned before, it is not the neuron that falls in love, decides to go this way or that, be hopeful or disappointed, be giving and sacrificing or not, and it is not the neuron that makes up jokes; no command circuit or logic circuit can create jokes or devise funny things, and so on.

All the various activities of mankind are directed from beyond his physical body and through his other existing bodies. The energy system that nourishes these bodies works quite differently from that of the physical body, and their structure is not within the world of man's physical senses and perception; however, in the past few decades through technological advances and with the aid of photography, man has been proven to have other existential dimensions, which were scoffed at and regarded as mere superstition a few decades before. The following charts show the relationship between several important human bodies in a very simple format, picturing the author's perception and revelations.

Mental Body or Mind (Zehn) (The Management Body)

The mental body itself consists of several subdivisions (Figure 27). Each subdivision in turn can be considered as a separate body. These include the following:

- Memory and Archive of the Eternal Data
- Memory Management
- Data-Arranging Management (Creating Thoughts)
- Cell and Body Management

Mental Body is a management that organizes different sections and generally consists of the below subdivisions. However each subdivision, in turn, has its detailed subsets. The following are the main subdivisions:

- Cell and Body Organization
- Human Perception Organization
- Data Organization (the eternal data archives)

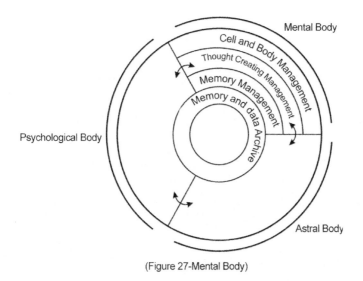

(Figure 27-Mental Body)

Here we raise a question, "What factors cause the body management to assign a false command and duty description to a cell or a group of cells, and, for example, cause a cell to become hyperactive (cancer), or hypoactive (atrophy)"

The answer lies in the fact that a great part of the body's energy management is being wasted. The reasons for this waste of mental energy are:

> •The excessive involvement of the Mind (Zehn) with matters which have nothing to do with the person and have no impact on his life.

> •The human Mind coming into conflict with the unity of the universe, disintegrating and fragmenting it through bias, and creating discrimination and multiplicity, which in turn wastes a great deal of mental energy.

Sohrab Sepehri, clearly expresses this in his poem;

I don't know

Why some say that the horse is a noble animal,

And that the pigeon is beautiful

And why no vulture dwells in any person's cage?

I wonder why the clover is inferior to the rose.

One must wash eyes, and look differently at things.

Words must be washed.

The word must be the wind itself,

The word must be the rain itself.

Since man's mental energy is limited, a plan and programming titled *Mental Energy Management* (a separate book from the author) is required for spending this energy. One of the issues discussed in *Mental Energy Management* is the amount of wasted mental energies. For instance, consider a pedestrian who is passing by a pavement while speculating on every other pedestrian. He evaluates them based on their looks and appearance (being overweight or underweight, beautiful or ugly, short or tall and so on), their overt and covert characteristics (being kind, wicked, and so on) [and even their hidden thoughts]. He judges them accordingly, for no apparent reason, benefit, or purpose. These [unnecessary] assessments consume and waste a tremendous amount of mental energy. As a result the mental management becomes exhausted and disturbed that leads to mismanagement of the body.

Psycheal Body or Psyche

The psycheal body is another important body of man's existence that detects, examines, and displays the emotions. It does not examine any of the consequences gained on the Step of Eshq and sends the related messages to the brain, which in turn reveals the necessary reactions on the physical body. A horror scene for example, first passes through the world-viewing filter of the mental body which determines its intensity. That is why a scene that is considered terrifying for an individual might not be so scary for another. Similarly, one woman might be terrified and even faint upon seeing a mouse whereas another woman might react normally. In any case, after the external events have been evaluated, the brain reacts and through its chemical messages makes the physical body to react accordingly.

That is to say that [in case of fear], first we are frightened by an external event, then a chemical secretion (in this case adrenalin) puts our body on alert, and consequently the relevant signs appear [on our face and body]. Or when we are deeply saddened by an external event, the brain receives the message and in turn sends out the associated chemical message. As a result the signs of depression appear.

As illustrated in Figure 28, the psycheal body is composed of two positive and negative sections with the following functions:

The positive section detects and perceives our positive emotions, and is in charge of the absorption and emission of the positive emissions. In other words when experiencing positive feelings, on the one hand the brain produces the relevant [positive] chemical messages; on the other, the positive section of our psyche emits positive emissions. In this case if the individual is exposed to [other people's] positive emotions, this section of the psyche also absorbs such positive emissions.

An individual who is using the positive part of his psyche, is idiomatically said to be in the **"Positive Phase"**, whereby he can only emit or absorb positive emissions.

The negative section discovers negative feelings such as anger, revenge, hatred, greed, jealousy and displays them. As a result of negative feelings, on the one hand, the brain carries out the relevant response on the body and produces toxins, on the other, the negative section of our psyche produces negative emissions which we expose others and ourselves to; in this state we are idiomatically in the **"Negative Phase"**.

At every possible moment, we can only use one of the sections of our psyche; the positive or negative section, and we can either be in the positive phase or in the negative phase. Upon being present in the negative phase, the imaginary valve to the positive one is automatically locked and the flow of emissions only happens through the negative phase. On the contrary, upon being present in the positive phase, the door to the negative phase is automatically locked and the positive door is only open. In other words this imaginary valve constantly blocks one of the positive or negative sections. Therefore depending on which of the positive or negative sections of our psyche that is blocked at the time, the individual will be deprived from (the emission or absorption of) its emissions.

Our thoughts, actions, and behaviors [hold and] emit their relevant emissions. For instance, when we look at someone with affection, he is bombarded with positive emissions, whereas looking at someone with anger and rage exposes the individual to negative emissions, and, as we will later discuss, this causes impairments in the individual; in a way that received emissions can even affect one's life expectancy (Life Span).

If a negative emission is directed towards us while we are in the positive phase, it will not penetrate us, as the door to the negative section of our psyche is blocked. However, if we are in the negative phase, this emission can readily penetrate and affect us. The reverse holds true as well; if a positive emission comes on our way while we are in the negative phase, it cannot penetrate us, as the positive section's door is blocked, and we will be deprived of it. *Therefore, we must try to maintain our mood in the positive phase as much as possible to prevent being affected by negative emissions.*

Positive or negative emissions are not a function of the dimensions of place [and time]; therefore, the person's far or near distance does not effect and change the intensity of the emissions.

There is a section in man's psycheal body that determines his life span, which we call, the "Life Span Coefficient". Therefore the more one receives or emits positive emissions; the higher is the life span coefficient and the longer he may live. Jesus Christ's (peace be upon him) famous motto "to love one's enemies" is based on this; one is far more hurt and damaged by being in the negative phase than can be imagined.

There are other human software that evaluate the positive and negative energies one receives:

•Under each mood (emotional state), man is always exposed to a kind of energy which he either receives or loses. For instance when we are praised, we receive a type of energy and as a result we even forget our feelings of fatigue or hunger, and we may even need less sleep. On the contrary, when we are blamed or criticized we lose this energy, feel downhearted and weak, and may be even unable to move.

This is the underlying basis of psychological war; where the enemy soldiers' morale is shattered with false news, in an attempt to convince them that they cannot win the battle, and by hurting the soldiers' national and military pride, their resistance is lowered.

•There is another software that measures our degree of happiness or dissatisfaction, and receives or loses energy accordingly. For instance after buying a second hand car, if a friend tells us that we have paid too much for it, we may feel discharged of energy and might even run a fever and become bedridden. At the same time, if someone else tells us that we made a real bargain and the car was worth the price, we might feel so overjoyed that we might stay awake all night not feeling tired. This is due to the effect of the above mentioned energy.

•Another software is in charge of "Self-assessment", therefore, feeling popular, loved and respected plays a great role in this process.

•There is also another important software which evaluates our feelings of guilt or good-deed (vices and virtues). This software gives (positive or negative) points to our feelings, and subsequently absorbs or repels energy. When energy is lost, our immune system acts weak and we are more susceptible to diseases.

•One's desires and needs are measured by another human software. Once not fulfilled, due to the software's low rating, we start to lose energy. On the contrary, in case of fulfillment, energy is gained and we feel uplifted.

•Another human software is "Goal-orientated software" which also gains or loses energy by evaluating us. For example, at the beginning of a football match all the fans -either those watching the game on TV or the ones present at the stadium- are in rather similar moods. However at the end of the game the winning team has absorbed a lot of energy and is capable of running for kilometers, whereas the supporters of the losing team have lost energy, do not have energy to talk, and feel extremely frustrated and downhearted due to losing this type of energy.

In fact, reaching one's ideal goals produces a particular energy in the individual that he totally forgets the fatigue and struggle he went through. Otherwise, the feeling of tiredness grows. This is why doing the same task over twice [without reaching a goal] consumes more energy and leads to more fatigue.

The overall gained and lost energies are ultimately evaluated by a master software that determines **the coefficient of life span or the coefficient of cellular fatigue.** In general, the more positive energy received, the greater the coefficient and the longevity. Conversely, more negative energy decreases life span and the longevity. Therefore, maintaining a positive phase has a great impact on our health.

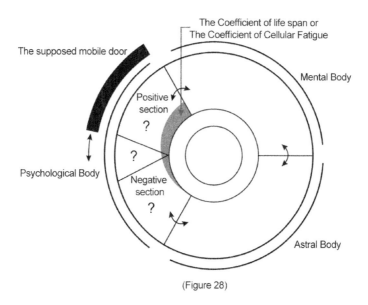

(Figure 28)

The Life Span Coefficient

As shown in Figure 28, the shaded section begins from the negative section (minimum intensity is in this section) and it increases in intensity as it moves toward the positive section. The illustrated section is called the Life Span Coefficient. It shows how our life span increases as we use more of the positive section and how it is reduced when we use more of the negative section. Thus, we can conclude that staying in the positive section is an important factor in increasing longevity.

Astral Body

The astral body is in charge of the two following main functions (Figure 29):

- •Directing anatomical growth

- •Conducting the messages of the secondary nervous system

Anatomical growth is the manner in which the cells are formed and arranged beside each other so that the growth continues from the embryonic stage toward the completed stage, and later on, the reconstruction and repair [that continues after birth].

The astral body also serves as a secondary nervous system conducting the messages of the secondary nervous system. It means each of the messages of the nervous system sent from the brain to particular cells or tissues are conveyed through both physical nervous pathways and the astral body. The astral body operates exactly like when sending a package to a place by post and simultaneously informing the receiver by phone or wireless that a parcel or message is on the way; therefore, the receiver of the message is ready to receive it and even knows what the package contains.

One of the functions of the astral body is the consistency of movements (e.g., of the limbs) that is due to the high speed response of different sections of the physical body to the orders sent out by the astral body.

Another function of the astral body is the physical body's quick response. Via especial exercises we can render the secondary nervous system more active which is used in martial arts, where they use the secondary nervous system in practice without knowing the mechanism of the astral body.

After seeing an event, a time lapse of approximately 0.3 seconds is required for decision-making and then taking action. However in martial arts some movements are performed in a much shorter time. In Japanese fencing, for example, the interval between attack and defense is extremely short and without any thinking. In martial arts, the coach's instructions emphasize actions based on sensing without thinking. Thinking actually has no place in martial arts, and the trainee exercises in such a way that his body parts themselves instantaneously show the appropriate reactions against the attacks; thus, he learns to react immediately to attacks without thinking. It is noteworthy that in Japanese fencing, a hundredth of a second can mean life or death. There is no chance to think and decide in such a short time. However the question is that do body parts have a brain of their own to react instantaneously to attacks?

The answer to this question, from the *Faradarmani* point of view, is that the **secondary nervous system** without the necessity of the primary (physical) nervous system can almost instantly elicit the appropriate response from the body parts.

Some might assume that **the automated division of** the subconscious (detailed description on page 225), which controls some automatic actions such as typing and driving, is in charge of this phenomenon. However, it must be noted that this automated system accomplishes and controls only certain well-defined and limited-ranged movements, whereas in fencing, for example, movements are by no means limited and one might be hit from all different directions, unpredictably. In contrast, in activities such as typing, all movements are predefined by **the subconscious automated system software** and are therefore predictable.

Another phenomenon proving the existence of the astral body is revealed when an individual experiences sensations such as pain and tickling in limb or an organ long after it has been removed from the body, for instance an amputated limb. In medical terms, this phenomenon is called "phantom pain," and it may be explained by different theories[1], such as the patient being delusional and believing the limb still attached.

In martial arts by continuous extensive practice on the astral body, the sensory range and perception of the surroundings are expanded, to such extent that some practitioners can detect the slightest movements around them with closed eyes and react appropriately.

The secondary nervous system is responsible for feedback of body movements, without which all man's movements and speech would be performed in a broken manner, like those of robots.

1- In science little is known about the true mechanism causing phantom pain; current theories are based on altered neurological pathways and cortical recognition.

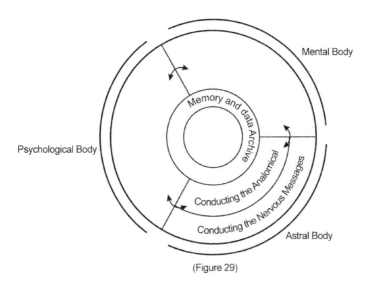

(Figure 29)

Death Types

According to Faradarmani's perspective, there are three different types of death:

1. Silent death

2. Physical death

3. Definite death

Silent death occurs when the aura of depression's negative energy takes over the human being's whole existence (Figure 25). In this case the human being suffers a breakdown in all perceptual communication, and while he understands the meaning of everything, nothing can motivate him. He becomes like a walking corpse, and is infected by the silent death.

Physical death happens when the heart stops, and the individual is medically considered (pronounced) dead[2], and the death certificate is issued. However, from the *Faradarmani* point of view, definite death has not yet occurred because the hundred trillion cells along with the mental body, psycheal body, astral body,

2- A precise medical definition of death, however, becomes more problematic, paradoxically as scientific knowledge and technology advance. Death was once defined as the cessation of heartbeat (cardiac arrest) and of breathing, however, this is now called "clinical death." Today, doctors and coroners usually consider death when the electrical activity in the brain ceases (cf. persistent vegetative state) which is called "brain death" or biological death. However, the determination of brain death can be complicated.

and so on, are still alive.

Definite death occurs when the astral body dies. Death of the astral body usually begins some minutes after the heart stops, and the astral body can survive even several days after the heart has stopped beating. As long as the astral body is alive, death is not yet definite, and the person may come back to life. Therefore **definite death occurs when the astral body dies.**

This phenomenon explains the instances throughout history and around the world where people have come back to life after physical death, even several days after their medically pronounced death or after being kept in the mortuary. From the medical point of view this concept would be considered impossible. Yet *as long as the astral body remains alive, any shock that stimulates it can cause the vital force to flow through the body once more, and the heart, although stopped for a while, begins to beat again and blood flows through the vessels without any coagulation.*

Nowadays, the concept of people coming back to life after the death certificate has been issued is considered a problem around the world. No scientific explanation has been yet proposed regarding this matter. However due to the frequency of such reports, there are debates for reconsidering the laws regarding the issuance of the death certificate. Defining new laws, such as keeping the corpse in the burial waiting room for a certain period under lawfully defined conditions, would allow the possibility of gaining more control over the situation.

After definite death, only the **mental body** survives and remains alive. This is the body that continues living in the space-less (or without the dimension of space) world. The mental body is the part that people often refer to as a ghost or spirit. During activities such as necromancy or communication with the deceased, it is actually the mental body of the dead person with which some people can establish a connection.

All the individual's information and experiences are recorded and stored with extreme accuracy in the mental body. Through hypnosis, it is possible to penetrate the very deep layers where this information is accessible.

Subconscious Mind

The human subconscious is a collection of software-based programs (Figure 30), and it includes several different divisions, such as:

- The programmed self (primary or initial personality)

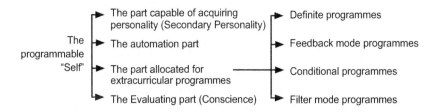

The programmable "Self"

- The part capable of acquiring personality (Secondary Personality) → Definite programmes
- The automation part → Feedback mode programmes
- The part allocated for extracurricular programmes → Conditional programmes
- The Evaluating part (Conscience) → Filter mode programmes

- The defensive self or the second mother: defensive psychological response

- The justice-attorney self: the High Court division

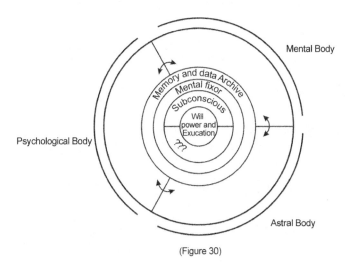

(Figure 30)

The Programmed Self

Every human being owns a unique software-based program upon birth. It is due to this program and its unique personal characteristics that each individual is entirely distinct from others. In this respect no two newborns ever have the same personality; as each owns an initial personality that he brings into the world with him.

Principles Governing the Human Being:

- Principle of pleasure-seeking
- Principle of avoiding pain
- Principle of obtaining results in the shortest possible time (hastiness)
- Principle of having limitless desires
- The principle of tendency towards Kamal (*Kamal*-seekingness):
- Principle of " Feeling Lost"
- The principle of distinguishing between good and evil
- The principle of self-awareness
- The principle of curiosity
- The principle of self-absorption (egocentricity):
- The principle of admiration-seeking
- The principle of seeking exclusive possession or monopoly
- The principle of self-interest (profit-seeking)
- The principle of stability for counter-reaction/reciprocal actions (aggressiveness, defensiveness, compromising)

During interaction with other human beings, other software become activated and the human being exhibits other reactions in defense of his self-centeredness. In fact, the above software strongly protect the individuals' egocentricity.

Secondary Personality

The secondary personality is also a section of the subconscious that is generally formed and programmed throughout childhood. The initial personality is shaped and patterned on the environment and finds its particular direction to form the secondary personality.

Automation Section

The model and pattern of all the human activities which are performed sequentially and repeatedly will eventually pass into the memory of a section called the "automated movements division" (automation). Subsequently without the need to think about the functions, they will proceed spontaneously.

For example, once a typist begins to learn to type, he encounters many problems in finding the position of each letter and spends a lot of time finding the locations of the letters on the keyboard. However, after a while, the subconscious memory learns the position of each letter, and the way the hands and the fingers position themselves will be stored in its software-based program. From then on, the typist will perform this function spontaneously, to such extent that it is not even necessary for the typist to look at the letters on the keyboard.

Miscellaneous Programs

A.Conditional Programming

The human being has been conditionally programmed in advance to different circumstances according to the construct: "If this …, then that …." This applies to many of his behavioral programs, and even to many of his illnesses. For instance, people are programmed during their childhood that 'if' they come out of the bath and sit in the wind, 'then' they will catch a cold, or 'if' their forehead is covered with sweat while being exposed to wind, 'then' they will experience sinusitis and so on. These examples are particularly applicable to Iranian culture, as each culture makes its own conditional constructs. These types of illnesses are called, software-based conditional illnesses.

B. Feedback-Based or Reactive Programming

A number of programs are definite, and the person continuously acts upon them. For example, consider someone who is told in his childhood that he is weak and he has to eat. With repetition of this statement, adults have programmed the child that he is weak so he has to eat, but they have not defined a limitation for it (until when must he continue to eat?). Consequently, now that the child has grown up and weights around 100 kilos, he is still attracted to food subconsciously and continues to eat non-stop. It seems as if he has another person inside him that eats the food. In old times, they used to call these "people with Jue" (literally meaning endless hunger, but it was considered as a type of disease). It was imagined there was a creature within them who eats the food!

Another example is a child who defecates on the carpet, and the parents chastise him for it. This program would enter his subconscious software, and when he is a grown up, he has chronic constipation. This programmed software inhibits him from the natural act of defecation. We call these types of illnesses, **the feedback or reactive software-based illnesses.**

C. Filter-based programming (beliefs)

Our beliefs are entered into this filter-based software. For instance, an individual in his childhood has been told to be rational and logical, and this statement has been repeated to him over and over again. In this way, the adults program this software based on pure solid logic (In Farsi there is an expression for this: "2x2=4 programming").

Afterwards, in his adulthood, this person cannot understand any subject outside the routine of logic and reasoning. Therefore, for such a person it would be very difficult to comprehend metaphysical matters, because this software-based filter blocks the entrance of many other programs and does not permit the entrance of information outside its defined boundaries. In summary, our beliefs are programmed in this section and they prevent the entrance of any type of information that is outside its program.

The Defensive (defending) Self or the Second Mother
(Defensive Psychological Response)

The defensive self is one of the most important sections of the subconscious. It enables the person to adapt to the environment and considerably reduces momentary stresses and anxieties. However, this defense in the majority of cases does not follow logic and is a form of self-deceit and escaping from the truth, very similar to a mother who is defending her child [on the principle that the ends justify the means]. Therefore despite all its necessity, the defensive self often harms and creates loss for the individual.

The defensive self defends a human being thoroughly and in all aspects, similar to a mother who in defense of her child would not consider many matters as she should, such as fairness and justice, righteousness or unrighteousness, and only thinks of getting her child out of the dangerous situation, so does the defensive self. In other words the defensive self acts like the friendship of a false (insincere) friend most of the time.

In order to defend the person, the defensive self provides the following services:

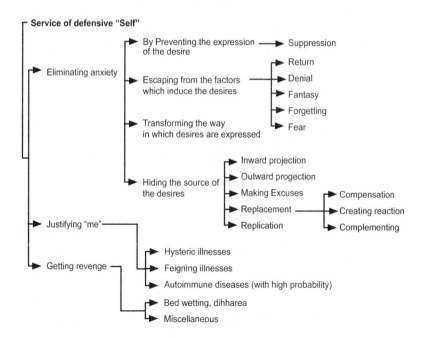

The Justice-Attorney Self or the High Court

The High Court is another division of the subconscious that takes action based on a **special self-assessing system**, and punishes those who are not acting in accordance with their responsibilities.

This court -in response to the negative potential energy which an individual produces; the **negative potential energy** of agitation, frustration, worry, bottled up feelings, and so on- brings him to the court and sentences him to bear the illness. These types of illnesses are called **psychosomatic illnesses or psyche-body illnesses.** In Faradarmani, considering the above explanation, we call this group of illnesses the **court-related** illnesses.

Under no circumstances are the convict's defenses acceptable in this court, as the court acts in accordance with the philosophy of the human being's creation. The belief of this court is that the human being has not come onto the Earth to produce negative potential energy.

The negative potential energy is the collection of the negative energies produced as a result of feelings such as agitation, frustration, worrying, bottled up feelings, sorrow and grief, sadness and unhappiness, eating one's heart out, feeling unfulfilled, feeling failure, feeling guilty, and so on.

One of the most important factors in creating the negative potential is **dual** or **two-faced behaviors** which include:

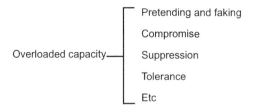

The **two-faced behaviors:** Two-faced behaviors compose a major part of our behaviors and help us adapt to the environment and our surroundings. However, when this is beyond an individual's capacity, it leads to the making of negative potential energy and eventually to psychosomatic illnesses. The High Court brings the negative potential energy case to court, and in proportion to the quantity of this energy, the individual is sentenced to suffer a type of illness. This illness can come with or without physical symptoms.

In summary, while interacting with the outside world events, an individual must often exhibit two-faced behaviors to better adapt to his environment. As this behavior is not favorable or desirable for him, it can consequently lead to agitation, frustration, bottled up feelings, and so on, followed by the accumulation of a type of negative energy called **the negative potential energy.** When the quantity of such negative energy reaches a certain level, the individual will be taken to the High Court and goes through a one-way conviction. The reached [guilty] verdict is executed on the individual as a physical illness, which sometimes has no specific physical symptoms, yet one feels the pain and the related disabilities. As this type comes with no physical symptoms, the medical doctor would tell these patients that their problems are stress related, or more specifically, that they have psychosomatic illnesses.

The basis of the High Court affairs, as we explained earlier, is a unique self-rewarding system that prosecutes individuals who neglect to fulfill their mission of attaining *Kamal*. It seems that this system is in accordance with the whyness of the human being's creation and his *Kamal*, since it causes him to understand that he has been created for greater purposes, rather than agitation, sorrow, tribulation, and so on. In the High Court, none of our justifications or our reasons for creating the negative potential energy will be accepted.

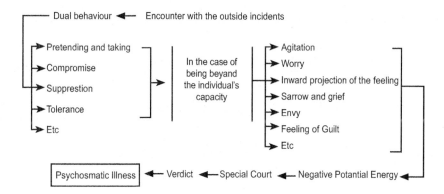

Below are several of the common illnesses related to the High Court:

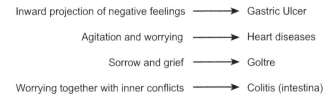

Inward projection of negative feelings ⟶	Gastric Ulcer
Agitation and worrying ⟶	Heart diseases
Sorrow and grief ⟶	Goltre
Worrying together with inner conflicts ⟶	Colitis (intestina)

Definition of the Logic Filter

This software protects the individual against the entrance of irrational and illogical information. In this way, it controls the functionality of the body's management, which is the Zehn, by monitoring the entering information. Entrance of false information, leads to it being implemented on the individual that can be dangerous in some instances.

The logic filter has two subdivisions:

•The conscious section, which is located at the consciousness level. The individual is aware of its framework and attempts to use it con sciously. Being logical and rational has been defined differently for each individual, and this software has been programmed, including both right and wrong programs, in the name of logic. The individual uses it for his decision-making and choices.

•The unconscious section, which involuntarily blocks **the entrance of information** into the human's Zehn, and protects the Zehn's management from the entry of false data. After examining the data for being in accordance with the rational standards and logical beliefs which the person has acquired throughout his life, it will then allow the information to pass into other subconscious areas.

For instance, while encountering difficulties in the living environment, if somebody gets angry and says, "I cannot see this anymore," the conscious section of his logic filter can precisely understand what he means: he wants a change in the situation, and this does not mean he wants to become blind. If the same statement enters the unconscious section of his logic filter, wishing "not to see" will also not be considered as "wanting to become physically blind". However if, with the slightest possibility, this section is convinced that wishing "not to see" means "wanting to become physically blind," this section will take action, and the command will enter the "willpower and execution" division. Consequently the wish is implemented through the management of the body and the cells, and this management orders the person not to see from now on; thus, **hysteric blindness** would occur. That is to say, in spite of the eyes being physically healthy, the individual cannot see.

Definition of the Subconscious Filter

There is another filter located in the subconscious, which consists of the entire set of logical or illogical information and beliefs which are the product of the individual's life. It also includes the information which the individual has developed a clear mental attitude toward, or the data that his family or society and environment have programmed into him.

This section puts a filter in the way of information entering the subconscious. If that information is not in accordance with the filter's data, it refuses them and does not allow them in. However, if the filter accepts them, such information will then enter into the "willpower and execution" division, and it will be definitely implemented.

The subconscious software of all human beings is programmed in a special way so that it considers certain things subconsciously possible and other things impossible. Therefore, when dealing with the outside world, these filters reject some of the incoming information [and consider them as impossible]. For instance, when this software is programmed entirely based on logic and reasoning, it strongly rejects all subjects outside this category.

Definition of the Will Power and Execution Division

After the subconscious filter approves certain information, it sends it to the "willpower and execution division" for the information to become implemented.

166 HUMAN, from another outlook

For example, if an individual wishes to walk on fire, the subconscious filter strongly resists this entry (information) and prevents such information from reaching the willpower and execution section. Therefore, under no circumstances, does the individual accept to step on fire, and if he does, he will be burnt badly. However, after several years of constant practice and by changing the program of this filter through suggestions and self-hypnosis, one would be able to step on fire in such a way that he would not only not feel the heat, but also be able to feel cold while on the fire.

The reason that the cells do not become damaged is that they do not receive any order from the mental body to react to burning. Consequently, the cells can function easily under such circumstances, in the same manner that some creatures [and plants] living in 250° Centigrade temperature and under the immense pressure at a 2500 meter depth do. While these creatures have the same cellular structure as human cells, they live in such conditions without difficulty or being damaged because the duty description of their cells has been defined for such environmental conditions.

Definition of Hypnosis

The crossing of information (suggestion) through the logic filter into the subconscious, followed by passing through the subconscious filter into the willpower and execution center, creates a condition called hypnosis.

Although in definitions of hypnosis it is said that if the information reaches the subconscious, hypnosis takes place, however *Faradarmani* has a different point of view: the incoming information must also pass the software-based programs of the unconsciousness. Based on this, hypnosis-susceptibility [hypnotizability] or hypnosis-insusceptibility [non-suggestibility] can be defined as follows.

The Common Definition of Hypnosis

Information (suggestion) ⟶ Logic Filter ⟶ Subconscious ⟶ Hypnosis

The Definition of Hypnosis in Faradarmani

Information (suggestion) → Logic Filter → Filter of subconscious programs → Willpower and execution center → Hypnosis

Definition of Suggestibility [Hypnosis-Susceptibility]

As we have learned, the software-based program of the subconscious has been programmed based upon the entered information throughout a person's lifetime, especially in childhood. All the information and incoming programs are compared with this filter, and they can only enter if they conform to it.

Suggestibility is defined as lack of resistance of this software-based filter to the incoming programs and information. For instance, someone whose subconscious software has been programmed during childhood and adulthood only based on logic and reason, when encountering subjects outside that logic and reason such as metaphysical and *Fara-zehni* (Ultra-mental) matters, resists accepting them. Therefore, such information cannot pass through his subconscious and will not reach the willpower section to be executed. Example: During hypnosis, the individual, also called "'the subject," is told through suggestion that his eyelids are getting heavier and heavier. However as the software-based program of his subconscious begins to analyze and interpret this message, it cannot find a reason for the eyelids to become heavier, and so it does not approve this message. Thus, the hypnotist's continuing suggestion is useless.

Or the same applies to when the hypnotist suggests to the subject that his hands are getting lighter. Again, the subject's software compares this statement to its own subconscious program, which states that whatever exists within the Earth's gravity field cannot become lighter. Therefore, the software judges the suggestion as impossible, and again the hypnotist's suggestions are ineffective. Such people are referred to as **"non-suggestible** [hypnosis-insusceptibility]."

In contrast, people whose subconscious software assumes everything is possible and permits the incoming information to pass through are called **"Suggestible."** Without suggestibility, no one can be hypnotized, and the hypnotist's efforts would be fruitless. In fact, in hypnosis, the subject determines the result of the hypnosis, not the hypnotist.

Classification of Individuals

People react differently when encountering matters that they have not experienced before or about which they have no information. Based on their reactions, we can divide people into two general categories:

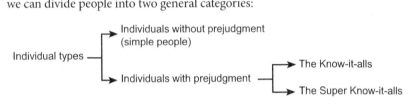

Individuals without Prejudgment:

Such people have no prejudgment or bias toward new information and what they do not know. Their opinion, comments, and judgment is subject to testing, doing research and making inquiries. They explicitly, with courage and bravery, admit to things they do not know about and have not experienced before. Overall, when they do not have sufficient information about a subject, they will not prejudge it; however, if they were to express their opinion, they would first try or test the subject, and only then state their opinion. **These are, as a matter of fact, researchers without prejudice, that is, "simple" people.**

In the Farsi language the true meaning of a simple person has not been properly defined. People often misuse and confuse this word with concepts such as "naïve or simple-minded." However, here, "simple" has the meaning that Jesus Christ (peace be upon him) describes in the Bible: "Unless you change and become as simple as little children, you will never enter the kingdom of heaven."[3] **This group benefits the most from Divine mercy.**

Individuals with Prejudgment:

3- At that time the disciples came to Jesus and asked, "Who, then, is the greatest in the kingdom of heaven?" He called a little child to him, and placed the child among them. And he said: "Truly I tell you, unless you change and become like little children, you will never enter the kingdom of heaven. Therefore, whoever takes the lowly position of this child is the greatest in the kingdom of heaven. And whoever welcomes one such child in my name welcomes me. (Matthew 18)

As soon as they encounter a new subject, without having sufficient information or knowledge, such people immediately express their opinion and easily judge and make assumptions. These people are further divided into two groups:

The Know-it-alls:

They have presumption and prejudgment of literally everything, and they are opinionated about every subject. However, in the end they are still willing to stop prejudging, and to test, analyze and investigate the matter without prejudice (like a researcher), and so postpone the announcement of their final verdict until they have tested and researched into it.

The Super Know-it-alls:

They think that they know all the knowledge and science in the universe and that there is nothing in the entire universe beyond the boundaries of their knowledge and wisdom.

They always compare [and judge] everything within their own archive of information, experience, and knowledge. If something is completely in accordance with this archive, then it is considered to be true; otherwise, the matter is definitely impossible. However, considering the sheer size of the universe, the culmination of all the wisdom, science and knowledge of all human being's throughout history, cannot approximate even a fraction of the entire universal information. A true thinker knows very well that the more he knows, the more he questions, and the more his unawareness and ignorance become apparent. As Avicenna[4] says:

My knowledge advanced high enough to understand

How ignorant I am!!

Or as Abu Saeed Abil Kheir says:

Although my heart much sought in this vast land [of creation],

it did not find a thread (it didn't get to know even the tiniest bit),

in spite of much details that it explored.

4- Ibn Sina (980 CE), commonly known in English by his Latinized name Avicenna, was a Persian polymath and the leading physician and philosopher of his time.

From my heart rose thousands of suns,

Still could not reach the mystery of the Kamal of a tiny particle.

This group throughout all the centuries have obstinately opposed and acted as a brake on new subjects and phenomena, and strongly resisted any new or innovative idea. It is said of these people:

"Deaf, dumb, and blind, they will not return (to the path)"

- Quran; Baqarah: 18

In world of *Erfan* it is considered better to avoid wasting time with such people, and they are referred to by different terms. Hafez says:

Don't tell the secrets of Eshq and divine drunkenness to an arrogant,

Let him die ignorantly, in his pain of egoism and self-worship.

Or:

Don't talk about the secrets of the universe to the concealed (those who do not want to be exposed to the truth)

Don't speak of the soul to the (lifeless) painting on the wall.

Finally, *Rumi* when describing the story of Jesus (peace be upon him), in the 3rd book of *Masnavi*, has called this group "fools":

"The greatest name (of God) and the miracles which I chanted to the deaf and the blind,

became effectual.

/ recited those words to the rock-hard mountain,

It became split, tearing the covering robe down to the navel.

I pronounced those words over a dead body,

it came to life.

I pronounced them over a non-entity,

it turned into an entity.

I said those words a hundred thousand times,

with loving-kindness to the heart of the fool

Not in the slightest, it was a cure.

Therefore, escape from fools just as Jesus did

For a fool's companionship has shed so much blood.

Or in another poem he says:

Playing music for the deaf is a waste of talent

and a handsome man sharing a house with the blind pointless.

Chapter Four

The Positive Network and the Negative Network

Don't tell the secrets of Eshq and divine drunkenness to an unaware,

Let him die ignorantly, in his pain of egoism/self-worship.

-Hafez

The human being's journey toward *Kamal* is influenced by two networks: the positive network and the negative network. The positive network provides all the necessary awareness and information for reaching *Kamal*; conversely, the negative network provides all the information and awareness that can distract and distance one from the path toward *Kamal* [*Kamal*-thwarting network].

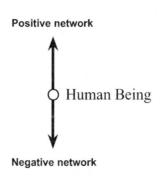

(Figure 31)

Without the existence of such a hindering force, journey toward *Kamal* would fail to provide the necessary values, because there would be no need to exert effort or strategies to reach *Kamal*[1].

And so, the human being is constantly dealing with two forces and attractions; one is toward spirituality and *Kamal*-seeking, and the other is the anti-*Kamal* or *Kamal*-thwarting force.

The Law of Reflection

Each moment every human being has a reflection from his being, resulting from his thoughts, words, and deeds. This reflection that can be positive or negative, is reflected into the upper world and passes through a filter that evaluates the human being's capacity and capabilities.

("On no soul doth God place a burden greater than it can bear"

-Quran; Baqarah: 286)

This filter determines an appropriate reflection, negative or positive, that conforms to the framework of justice [and the person's capacity], and subsequently refers this reflection to the positive or the negative network to be implemented on the individual.

("God leads to stray whom He wills, and guides whom He wills"

- Quran; Nahl: 93)

For instance, in the Quran, God says about the negative reflection that He himself assigns a demon to such individual:

"If anyone neglects the Divine Mercy,

we appoint for him a devil, to be an intimate companion to him"

- Quran; Zukhruf: 3

The reflection, when executed, first amplifies the individual's original reflection, and second, it brings about a positive or a negative awareness for the individual that is consistent with his original reflection. Consequently, it either truly

---

1- Necessity of human's free will to choose between the negative and positive network.

guides the human being or misleads him. Thus, a stingy person is most likely to become more [and not less] stingier over time, a malicious person becomes more malicious, or the aware person becomes more aware.

In view of the Law of Reflection, we can well understand how this verse: *"God leads to stray whom He wills, and guides whom He wills"* (Quran; Faatir.8) is implemented through the negative or positive networks, how the guidance or the misleading of man is arranged; one becomes under His guidance, or the demon is assigned to him.

The simple diagram below illustrates the relationship between human beings, God, and the Negative and Positive Networks.

Below you will find more detailed explanation on the awareness of the positive and negative network:

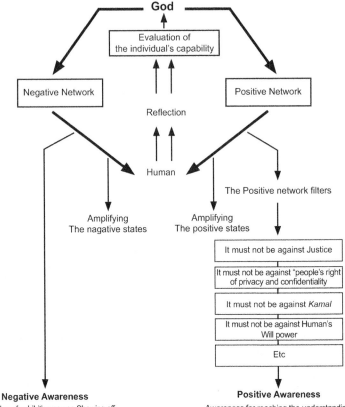

God

Evaluation of
the individual's capability

Negative Network

Positive Network

Reflection

Human

The Positive network filters

Amplifying
The nagative states

Amplifying
The positive states

It must not be against Justice

It must not be against "people's right
of privacy and confidentiality

It must not be against *Kamal*

It must not be against Human's
Will power

Etc

Negative Awareness

knowledge of exhibiting power, Showing off,
guidiness

Gaining superiority and dominance over others

*Reaching the materialistic and earthly profits and
goals, personal gains*

Positive Awareness

Awareness for reaching the understanding,
perceiving and knowledge of *Kamal*

*Understanding the Whyness of being and the
mystery of the creation, finding the significance of
an individual's being*

**Result of
Navigate Awareness**

How to gain power:

Power to exert influence on others

Power of mind reading

Power to foresee the future (Fortune telling)

Power to tell / read people's personality

Etc

**Result of
Positive Awareness**

Understanding, perceiving and knowledge of
Kamal:

Perception of the Unity of the world of existence
as a whole

Understanding "I am God"

Understanding the magnificence of the Beloved

Understanding the purpose of creation

Etc

Filtering the Awareness that are in Violation of Justice

The positive network never [in no circumstances] provides the kind of awareness that violates the **Divine justice**. For instance, if the positive network reveals awareness of the exam questions to a student, this opposes justice; thus, such a thing certainly does not occur via the positive network.

Therefore, if somebody can perform such actions, it is obvious that he has received this kind of awareness only from the negative network; the positive network would definitely not pass such information to anyone.

Filtering the Awareness that are in Violation of "Sattar-al-Oyoub" (Fault-Veiling) The Positive Network and Filtering the Awareness that is in Violation of Personal Privacy and Confidentiality ("Sattar-al-Oyoub")

The positive network itself is *"Sattar-al-Oyoub"*[2], and covers all the individuals' flaws. Therefore, it is impossible for the positive network to provide anybody information about other people's personalities and their faults. Thus, if somebody receives such awareness regarding other's personality that reveals or allows one to read people's [hidden] faults, this information is undoubtedly from the negative network.

Only God is aware of the nature of the humans (*"God knoweth well all the secrets of the hearts" -Quran; Al-e-Imran: 119*). It is for this reason that the right of judgment about other human beings is absolutely reserved for God and no one else, because all of man's judgments are imperfect and at a superficial level [subjective].

Filtering the Awareness that are in Violation of Free Will

The whyness of man's creation [philosophy of creation] is based on the attainment of *Kamal*. Thus the factor that makes this journey to *Kamal* possible is man's freedom to choose. Without freedom of choice, people cannot assume responsibility, and so if man's free will is distorted, the spectacular design of

---

2- Literally means fault-veiling and is one of the names of God that literally means "one who covers the flaws," and in Erfan this term is used as "keeping people's right of privacy and their confidentiality".

creation would become entirely futile and pointless. The negative network therefore attempts to interfere in a human being's freedom of choice through various means. One of these is providing him awareness the use of which prevents him from using his own intellect and contemplation to choose his path, which removes the burden of "making choices" from man.

Since man, due to his indolence and strong desire to keep his personal interests, would also be eager to have an accompanying agent who, in addition to guaranteeing his personal interests, shows him all the paths so that he does not have to look into or evaluate them himself. Therefore, it is very tempting for humans to be relieved of the responsibility of contemplating and making decisions. In this regard, the negative network provides numerous services such as fortune telling, to strip man of his freedom to choose his own destiny and to make a weak-willed puppet out of him.

The positive network, in contrast, provides humanity with the general necessary awareness and guidance for the journey toward *Kamal*, but leaves decision-making and choosing which path to take at each moment, to the human being at his own discretion and free will. Therefore, what he should buy or sell, whom he should marry, whether he should divorce his spouse, and other similar two-way divergent paths will not be answered by the positive network, for the reason that, it is upon choosing between such divergent paths that the human being is tested. Essentially, life is composed of infinite two-way divergent paths, from choosing a pair of shoes to choosing your spouse and so on. And if we were supposed to be told what to buy, what to sell, and so on, then what is the role of humankind?

On the other hand, from the point of view of an observer located in the unipolar world[3], there are no time and space dimensions; therefore, there is no past and future. From this point of view, the universe has been created in zero time and has already ended; therefore, at that moment, all the information of past, present, and future appears in front of this observer in the unipolar world. According to this theory, the destiny of the human being is clear, but it is not im-

---

3- As previously mentioned from the point of view of an observer located in the dipolar world that we are currently living in, there exists contradiction and polarity, and the dimensions of time and space, whereas from the point of view of an observer located in the unipolar world, it lacks dimensions of time, space and contradiction or any other dimension (For details please refer to the book "Human's insight" from the same author).

posed upon him. Thus, whatever exists is the outcome of his free will, and he is not regarded as a powerless puppet.

Trespassing On Others' Being or Gaining Power Over Others (Mind-Reading or Charming By Using Magic)

Man's existence is a sacred territory and it is only here where God has breathed into him the essence of His Spirit. Thus, man's existence is "The House of God" or "*Baitollah*." Nobody has the right to intrude into this boundary, and one should approach it with reverence and respect.

One of Satan's [deceptive] weapons is breaking the sanctity of this boundary and intruding through various methods. To encourage people to do so, he has devised many beautiful justifications such as understanding people's problems, helping others, and similar justifications that prepare the individual to intrude and trespass on others' territories. After gaining such power and tasting its sweetness, the individual is attracted to it and will not let go.

Such people make others believe that this power is the result of Divine generosity and purity of their heart, which enables them to read people's minds or influence and gain power over them. Via such justifications they get ensnared in a satanic game that not only endangers other people's privacy but also ruins their own lives and entangles them in an action that brings no *Kamal*.

Trespassing on others has the following **satanic motivations**:

- Trespassing in order to exert one's personal will power and to charm people (by using magic). This in turn, has two purposes:

- Trespassing in order to suggest one's thoughts on the individual

- Trespassing in order to exert will power

- Trespassing in order to read people's minds

- Trespassing in order to read people's personalities

The Power of Reading (Perceiving) People's Personalities

Many disciplines encourage people to trespass on others and read their personality. For the reason that every human, without a doubt, has some personality faults and flaws of his own, this action only leads to separation of human beings from one another and pushes them into the world of Multiplicity, as *Hafez* says:

Whoever came to this world has a mark of fault

In the midst of such a tavern, one should not ask for a sober person.

In summary there is nothing of real value to be sought inside individuals. Therefore, we must learn to see others as God sees us, through fault-veiling, so that in turn our own faults remain unexposed.

Perception of "Ana-al-Haqq"[4]

"Baitollah" (the house of god) is exclusively used to refer to human being, given that it is the only place where in God has breathed the essence of His Spirit. *("And I (God) breathed into him of My spirit" - Quran; Al-hijr. 29)*

Thus, we must approach other individuals' boundaries with total inviolability and sacredness, and no human being has the right of intrusion there. Anyone who reaches such perception has indeed reached the perception of *"Ana-al-Haqq"* and is considered an intimate of the *"Baitollah."*

The Beloved, bestowed His own magnificence upon man,

Passed the secrets of His sanctuary to His befriended resident,

The cash in the universe's treasury,

The King bestowed with generosity to this particle in the universe.

-Hafez

Perception of the Unity (Wholeness) of the Universe

Perception of the unity (wholeness) governing the universe and that all the

---

4- "I am The Truth) God(." This legendary statement apparently led to "Mansour Hallaj's" -a Persian Sufi- long trial that consequently earned his public execution and martyrdom.   .

particles of universe are in close cohesion, connection and communication with each other is one of the objectives of the world of *Erfan*. In fact, the universe is integrated and unified; no constituent can exist without the existence of others. Yet the mystic sees this from another point of view, as he sees the universe as the manifestation and the image of the Beloved (God).

You are the mirror reflecting His magnificence,

And your reflection is indeed all the universe.

-Attar

Perceiving the Magnificence of the Beloved

In the world of Eshq, there is a principle that serves as a valuable yardstick for recognition of being in love: "The one in love finds the beauty and magnificence of the beloved faultless."

The *Leyli* and *Majnoon* story[5] teaches this lesson clearly to man. In the story, their love became a word of mouth and everyone assumed how beautiful Leyli must have been to have made Majnoon so crazy for her love, to such a level that he wandered about in the plains and deserts. Therefore, everybody was curious to see her, and finally the king summoned Leyli to his palace. He wanted to see her, face to face, to see the beauty that had created such a great love. However, when the king finally met Leyli he was amazed to find her quite an ordinary girl. Therefore, he told her, "Then it is you that have caused Majnoon to [madly] wander about in the deserts, but you are not prettier than the others?!" In response, Leyli unveiled the great truth: "It is the way Majnoon perceives me that has indeed caused such a passionate love and it his loving eyes that cannot see my flaws".

Someone who has such eyes as Majnoon's can pass through both worlds easily as he cannot see any fault in them.

The king said to Leyli, "So are you the one for whom Majnoon went insane

---

5- Leyli and Majnoon ("Leyla and The Madman") is a deep love story by the Persian poet Nezami Ganjavi. Qeys (Majnoon) falls in love with Leyli but there are obstacles parting them. Majnoon becomes obsessed with Leyli to the point that whatever he sees he sees as Leyli, for him everything is in terms of Leyli; hence he was called Majnoon (literally meaning possessed). Leyli and Majnoon resemble love stories such as Romeo & Juliet.

and out of his mind!"

Well, you are not fairer than other fair ones."

She replied, "Be silent, as you are not Majnoon.

If you were to have Majnoon's eyes,

You would pass the two worlds6 harmlessly. "

-Molana Rumi

A person in love reaches unity, and desires nothing except his Beloved. In fact through this experience of love, he reaches oneness and becomes a [true] Monotheist and seeks nothing but his Beloved. No matter what he sees, nothing will distract him from his Beloved. Indeed one of the aims of earthly love is to reach such perception:

Keep quiet and don't grieve too much

As a self in love, cannot be a malicious self [tempting him to wrong-doing and distracting him from the right path]

-Molana Rumi

Perception of His Presence

The ardor and yearning of His lovers for His union, brings about incomprehensible exaltation. We are travelling toward God through a path that returns us to Him (the path of *"Ilayhi-Rajioon"*: "and to Him we will return" Holy Quran). In this phase of life, [the experience of] joining Him is indeed the perception of His "Presence"7, higher than which a human cannot experience. Therefore, while we are within our physical body, the maximum level of union with God is reaching the perception of His presence.

6- This life and the afterlife.

7- There is no accurate description for this, because it is taking place at the step of Eshq in a world that is 'Free of Tools', therefore this concept is purely perceptual [such as the taste of an apple]. Nevertheless, it is rather 'witnessing His presence,' not the theoretical knowledge of it.

Understanding the Purposefulness of Creation

Understanding the purpose of creation is attaining the perception that creation is based on a purposeful design. As it is impossible to assume God taking useless and futile action, we thereby understand that the Creation has happened through a clever design and lofty purpose.

How to Distinguish between the Awareness of the Positive and Negative Networks

As is clear from the below diagram representing both networks, most of the power upon which a human being becomes attracted to and strongly pursues, spending years to achieve, are all offerings of the negative network. The positive network by no means makes even one such thing available to anyone because such powers contradict people's right of privacy and confidentiality *(Sattar-al-Oyoub)*, Divine Justice, human free will, and so on. Further, the positive network provides humanity with only awareness related to *Kamal* and nothing more.

Without a doubt, one of the sweetest experiences in the world of *Erfan* is receiving awareness. The emptiness of unawareness becomes filled with pure Divine awareness that comes with indescribable pleasure and can quench the thirst of a thirsty man. However, sometimes an individual -due to his raging thirst- may drink from any glass regardless of its content to quench such thirst, without noticing that the offered drink might be from the negative network.

All inspiration that human beings may receive, belongs either to the positive network or the negative network.

The information from the positive network guides man toward Kamal and facilitates his path in reaching oneness and unity with the universe. Among the outcomes of such guidance is attaining inner joy, peace, and so on.

Information that provides a means for showing off, attaining personal gains, gaining dominance and influence over others, mind-reading, and all information that contradicts God's justice and fault-veiling, violates man's freedom of choice, personal privacy and confidentiality (Sattar-al-Oyoub), and causes multiplicity, all come from the negative network. The positive net-

work never provides anyone with such information.

Among the outcomes of using -knowingly or unknowingly- the information received from the negative network are feeling anxious and restless, depression and disappointment, sorrow and grief, or loneliness and so on. In addition, all the information that induces fear and terror, worrying and stress, disappointment and hopelessness, sorrow, grief and depression, whether received while awake or asleep (dreams), are definitely from the negative network.

Awareness Coming From the Positive Network	Awareness Coming From the Negative Network:
• Awareness about the whyness of creation, the purpose and mystery of being, and the path towards Kamal	• Awareness regarding [methods of] gaining power and superiority over others
• The way of resolving one's conflicts and reaching unity (oneness) [with God, universe, self, and other people]	• Awareness in order to discover other people's faults and reading their personalities
• The way of attaining the perception of Kamal	• Awareness that encourages judging others
• Perception of the unity (oneness) of the whole universe	• Awareness that leads human being into the negative phase
• Perception of "Ana-al-Haqq"	• Awareness that directs man toward Multiplicity
• Understanding the magnificence of the Beloved	• Awareness in order to gain powers such as mind-reading, fortune-telling, exerting influence and charming others through magic, and so on.
• Perception of His Presence	
• Understanding the purposefulness of man's creation	• Awareness that empowers one's arrogance, egocentricity, selfishness, and so on.
• Creating hope, peace, security, joy and so on	• Feeling disappointed, fearful, anxious, lonely, sad, depressed (while awake or asleep)

Kamal Versus Power

The type of information and awareness that a human being can transfer (with him) to the next life[8] is the most important subject examined in the *Erfan-e Halqeh* (Interuniversal Mysticism). Devising a plan for travelling through the path of *Kamal*, which in *Erfan* is called *Seir-o-Soluk* [exploration and transformation or mystical journey], depends on how much we know about the path. Knowing exactly what is needed along the path saves time and helps us to prepare all the necessary things.

Therefore, it is necessary to have some information about the next lives, such as that our next (immediate) life continues in the space-less dimension. There, we lose the dimension of space [place, distance,..] and can be present everywhere at the same time, with only the dimension of time ruling us. Now, if we identify and classify the belongings of an individual, we can decide which category has use in the next life.

The first category of the belongings of an individual is earthly possessions such as science, powers, abilities, expertise, and all information that is required for day-to-day life, without which life would be difficult for human beings. This information and science is the result of an individual's lifetime achievement, such as the science of economy, the technique and skills in accountancy, knowledge of engineering a car or a computer, a building, an airplane and so on; none of the above mentioned groups has any use in the next life. **They are beneficial and effective in this life only if they lead the individual to perception and understanding of Kamal; otherwise, they are futile effort.**

In other words, we are taking part in an earthly game to gain experience in the hope of reaching the perception of different manifestations of *Kamal*. Therefore, none of the powers and capabilities gained through sport, exercise, and practice, such as weight lifting, skiing, jumping, the skills of typing, driving, or hairdressing is itself of any use in the next life. It is only the results gained from such activities that can help us in achieving our main goal of living this life. For example, we engage in sport and exercise to be fit, to stay healthy and to not become ill,

---

8- It should be noted that the next life refers to the life after human's physical lifetime on Earth, which is a world that lacks the dimension of place (space-less) and has no correlation at all with reincarnation.

so that we can explore the framework of *Kamal* more easily and thoroughly. We gain certain professional skills and qualifications to be able to earn a living, and in turn facilitate our search for answers to questions about our *Kamal*. Without such answers, our coming and going would be in vain.

The wind and the clouds, the sun and the moon and the sky are all in operation,

That you earn some bread, yet may eat it not in ignorance.

-Saadi

In general, human's "metaphysical possessions" include powers and abilities such as mind-reading, foretelling, reading others' personalities, and similar abilities, that despite the individual wasting years of his life acquiring them, none has any use in the next life. Another subdivision of human's metaphysical possessions is the knowledge of *Kamal* that includes all the awareness that is needed in the path of *Kamal*. As it will be discussed, this division is the only category of human possessions that is transferrable to the next life, and includes only *Kamal*-related perceptions such as Ana-al-Haqq, magnificence of the Beloved, Unity, and so on.

As we briefly explained before, none of the human being's earthly possessions [that are dependent on the dimension of space] are transferable to the next life; for example, a person's **knowledge and expertise** in economy, accounting, psychology, and computers and so on, has no value and no use in the next life. **These types of possessions are only used as realities in the current lifetime in order to make living possible, that in turn enables one to access a number of truths.** In the same manner, none of the **physical powers** has any use in the next life; for example, a weight lifter who can lift hundreds of kilograms or an athlete who holds records in jumping can apply none of such abilities in his next life. All such abilities in the current life serve to gain health and be fit so as to have a healthy body and longer life for the purpose of understanding the secrets and howness of Creation.

In addition, the supernatural powers such as fortune-telling, mind-reading, personality reading, and teleportation have absolutely no use in the next life; for example, if someone can teleport himself in this life, that power would be useless in the next life, since despite the individual spending years of his life acquiring them, there is no space dimension in the next life, and instantaneous teleportation is possible for everyone. The same applies to foretelling or reading others' minds and so on; all are possible for everyone in the next life; therefore, these powers have no value in the next life, and one is supposed to gain more valuable experiences than such matters in the next life. So we conclude that none of these powers are transferable to our next lives.

The second category of the belongings of an individual is the knowledge of Kamal, which is the only part of the human being's possessions that is transferrable to the next life and is considered our literacy in the next life. It contains perceptions of the unity (oneness), Ana-al-Haqq (I am the Truth/God), and other awareness available only through the positive network.

Therefore, the results of man's actions and the [final] thesis that human writes on the "game" of life is considered in total [and not based on each separate action]. This point requires an example to clarify what we mean by "results of actions." Suppose, to date, a student has scored zero for the spelling exam one hundred times. When he finally succeeds in achieving the maximum score, it does not matter how many times before he has gotten zero, because he has finally learned his lesson. Likewise is a student who has always scored the highest grade but scores zero in his final test. Accordingly, the final thesis and outcome of one's entire life is of primary importance and not the actions themselves. This final outcome is in fact the individual's level of *Kamal*-based perceptions and the outcome of his deeds.

Thus, we can summarize all the possessions of an individual into two main groups: **Kamal** and **Power. The conclusion is that only knowledge of Kamal is worth pursuing. Power in all its forms is perishable and wastes a human lifetime;** furthermore, it sometimes deceives an individual under the name of "a Divine gift", only to be at the service of the negative network.

Rumi likens power to candy and considers it a food for children. He suggests that we avoid eating it and wait until the main course, the perception of *Kamal*, comes along.

If you want to speak of words as sweet as sugar,

Wait. Don't be greedy, and don't eat from this Halva (candy).

Patience, is in the hands of the insightful,

Halva, only the desire of children's feast.

Those who are patient go beyond and above the world.

Those who eat Halva only sink distant from the goal.

-Molana Rumi

The true God-given grant [Vs. supernatural powers] to man is the collection of possessions that help human beings reach *Kamal*, that is, only the awareness and perceptions regarding the potential Divine ability. In other words, on the path to *Kamal* nobody is asked about the powers that they have, on the contrary, one is asked about the awareness and perceptions one has reached.

Definition of Enlightenment

Enlightenment means seeing lucidly and having clarity of vision about the universe and the whyness of creation: from where we have come, for what purpose we have come here into this life, where we are heading, and what purpose are we to achieve. Enlightenment means reaching an insight-viewing eye: The ability of perceiving wisdom and capability of reading the book of the universe that is the book of the apparent illuminating signs of God.

Enlightenment is the result of *Ettesal* and connection with the positive network and it is not something that one can falsely claim to have. One cannot achieve it through force [and effort], and it is achievable only through the world of *Erfan* and insight, revelation and illumination.

In some doctrines, the connection to the negative network is called enlightenment and used as means of showing off their powers and exerting their superiority over others. In this way, they mislead themselves and others. This has already been discussed in the "*Kamal* versus Power" and the "The Positive and Negative Networks" topics; however, we also briefly note them here again as it is a matter of importance:

•Anything that involves trespassing into the sacred [personal] boundary of others, such as mind-reading, charming, and so on.

•Anything that contradicts people's right of privacy and confidentiality and that reveals or allows one to read other people's personalities and their faults (*Sattar-al-Oyoub*), like personality-reading and revealing people's faults and secrets and so on.

•Anything that denies man's free will, such as the power of charming others through magic and so on.

•Anything that imposes incidents/fate upon an individual, such as black magic, spells and others.

•Anything that violates Divine justice, such as fortune-telling and so on.

•Anything that is achieved through working with **"anything that is not God"** or *Min Dun-e-Allah*, such as getting help from spirits or demons, Jinn (Non-organic creatures) and so on, instead of getting help from God, which is indeed breaking the promise of *"We ask help, only (and absolutely), from You "* -Quran; Faatihah:5.

Important Note: Those who are interested in *Kamal* and spiritual progress must have the necessary awareness for distinguishing *Kamal* from Power. They must well know the differences between these two in order to avoid falling into the trap of the negative network, as regaining freedom from such a trap is extremely difficult.

Definition of Science

Science is the study of the realities, finding the cause of the realities and the relationship between their different components. Reality is something that has occurred [exists] and has happened. Realities leave certain effects that can be tracked and are traceable, testable, recordable, storable, and repeatable. These effects can be divided into three general categories based on their traceability:

•The realities that are perceivable through the five senses.

•The phenomena that are recordable and can be studied only through special tools and instruments.

•The realities that do exist but have not yet been discovered.

Also, in regard to the cause of a reality's occurrence, the causes of some phenomena are clear and comprehensible for human beings, while some other cases are not. From the point of view of the methods of using and exploiting the realities in the world of science -whether the cause of an occurrence is known or not- the human being either has or does not yet have the facilities to make practical use and exploit them. An example of the first case (unknown cause) is the basis of the flight of airplanes, which is founded on "Bernoulli's principle." This principle states that in a streaming fluid, an increase in the fluid's speed leads to a decrease in pressure, and vice versa. Man has been using airplanes and helicopters for several decades without knowing the scientific basis of **Bernoulli's principal**. Thus, lack of knowledge of the causes and whyness of such phenomenon has not prevented and will not prevent man from using them.

> **Anything that has a reality and we can use and exploit in practice is considered as science, whether we know its cause or not. However, it is possible to know some things (realities) but do not wish to test them.**

Throughout history ignorant statements have sometimes been made, which have brought science considerable embarrassment and disgrace. For example, the report of the French Academy of Sciences against Dr. Franz Anton Mesmer[9] regarding hypnosis, wherein they called him a con artist and charlatan, and similar declarations about acupuncture, homeopathy, and so on.

History shows that many scientific achievements had initially been considered as unusual phenomena, unbelievable, and against the common knowledge and science of their time, and in some cases had been considered entirely as superstition. For instance, until some decades ago, if an aura was painted around the holy figures in religious paintings, the world of science considered it absolutely unreal and superstition. However, nowadays, through Kirlian photography technology, we know that each human being has a colorful aura around him.

9- Franz Anton Mesmer (May 23, 1734 – March 5, 1815) theorized that there was a natural energetic transference that occurred between all animated and inanimate objects that he called "animal magnetism" often called Mesmerism. The evolution of Mesmer's ideas and practices led to development of hypnosis.

Throughout history, instances have been reported of healers treating people only by placing their hands on the patient's body. This was definitely not acceptable previously in scientific societies, but several decades ago the map of the polarity field around the body was discovered in one of the United States' universities, and the effect of such a field on human health has been acknowledged. This discovery led to foundation of polarity therapy or energy therapy, and many people throughout the world have witnessed with their own eyes that treatment can take place through touching someone's head or body.

Therefore, if the world of science merely comments on or orally rejects an area of discussion it is not a criteria for its failure unless that judgment is based on valid experiments, documented tests, and research standards where by a subject (or hypothesis) is rejected and considered a failure. All innovations and novel ideas have initially faced such comments from the world of science. These oral comments are merely baseless and unofficial opinions, based on no proof or documentation, and are expressed without any research or investigation on the subject.

Every innovative concept in its era was faced with the non-scientific approach of the majority of the scholars. Instead of investigation, experiment, and taking into consideration the possibility of such concept [and considering the positive available results], they rejected and challenged the new idea only because it had no scientific recorded history. Nevertheless, all these confrontations finally led to the disgrace of the world of science. For example, such confrontation led to a two-century resistance against homeopathy. However, at last via numerous proofs in practice, today homeopathy is well known in the world, and its capabilities in diverse fields of treatment have been approved. Therefore, if this branch of treatment were under the protection and support of the scientific societies, it could have had a more prominent role in medicine and in our understanding of the human being and the nature of illness today. Certainly such resistance has postponed these benefits.

It is interesting to note that the world of science has a tricky way of opposing new ideas; upon encountering such innovations, it first denies them and resists them as much as possible, and it obstructs the progress of the idea and sabotages it. However, as soon as it comes across circumstances where it has to withdraw, it immediately changes its strategy, takes the matter into its own hands, and forms an academic framework for it in a manner wherein it pretends that it has discovered the innovative subject itself!

For example, let's consider acupuncture. First, the scientific world called it a fraud, then as they could not resist the practicality of acupuncture's results, they finally took the matter into their own hands and invented electro-acupuncture, in which electrodes are used to find the points of interest to carry out the required treatment. Yet it is entirely forgotten that until some decades ago, they made fun of this branch, and they thought of it as being fraudulent! Now they refuse to admit that they had made such comments about it.

The same applies to hypnosis, from which they have now developed hypnotherapy and present glorious reports and news about it, but they have never apologized to the memory of Franz Anton Mesmer. The scientific societies caused Dr. Samuel Hahnemann, who proposed the theory and practical basis of modern homeopathy, to die in poverty and misery. After realizing the importance of what he had done, he was gloriously reburied in Paris with great respect and praise. In this case at least, they acknowledged the embarrassment they had caused, but it came too late!

Indeed who would accept the heavy burden of these disasters and crimes of the scientific world? It will assuredly be the responsibility of those who have betrayed and will betray science as well as humanity, in the name of science itself.

Experience, Knowledge, and Questioning

All that man possesses through understanding, knowledge, and perception are the product of a triangle representing Experience, Knowledge or Science, and Questioning (Figure 32). At the beginning of man's journey, which of these three existed before the others and had been used by man [from the start]?

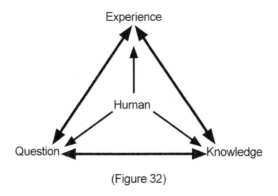

(Figure 32)

We might immediately respond that experience was the first thing humans encountered and became to know. It is certainly true that we have always encountered experience; however for an experience to become knowledge and learning, human beings must have already been equipped with a processing system that, with the help of the acquired experiences, enabled man to mentally process and finally reach certain conclusions that could then be called an experience. This processing system itself requires science, and without it no processing system can record and store any experience.

Therefore, we conclude that in order to benefit from experience, knowledge must have already existed. However, for knowledge to have been created, there must have been preceded unknowns and questions from which, after discovering their answers, knowledge and science be formed; therefore, without questions, there will be no answer and no science or knowledge, however the very process of answering a question in turn requires knowledge.

Yet if humans encounter no incidents, they raise no questions. Therefore, encountering an event causes man to think, which in turn raises some questions in his mind. In summary, without experience, no question can exist.

Thus, we encounter a paradox in which we cannot tell which angle of the above-mentioned triangle was created first. The only answer we may give is *that man is a unique being and with his own special abilities, he has accessed the three angles simultaneously from the very first beginning and has advanced them in parallel.* Indeed, this demonstrates the uniqueness of the human being among the infinite number of creatures on Earth.

Science and the Answer to the Mystery of Creation

Now we pose a question: Can the world of science find us an answer to the mystery of creation?

To answer this question we draw a diagram with a horizontal time axis against the vertical axis of number of man's questions.

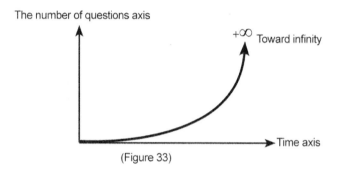

(Figure 33)

Figure 33 shows that at the beginning, man had only a few questions, but as he proceeded, his questions eventually grew into various branches of science. Each branch, in turn, has led to proposing more new questions, and as time has passed, the number of questions and the number of scientific branches has increased.

In recent decades, the number of questions raised has exceeded the total number of questions asked throughout the history of humanity. At this moment the circumstances are such that, though man has not yet found an answer for one question, hundreds of other questions arise from the new scientific branches , and soon man will reach a limit that we call **"the question crisis."** At this border of crisis, the ratio of new proposed questions to the answered questions rises daily and approaches infinity.

$$\frac{\textbf{Questions}}{\textbf{Answers}} = \textbf{Infinity}$$

At this border, human beings will permanently realize that science will never be able to create a condition where one day man can say, "I have found the answers to all my questions." All the Iranian mystics have understood this. And in spite of them being among the [greatest] scientists of their time, they expressed their disappointment in science and understood that it cannot give them the answer to the mystery of creation.

Talk to me of wine and the musician, and search less for the

secret of the universe.

No one found and shall find the pieces of this puzzle through

wisdom and skill.

-Hafez

The insignificances presented by science of geometry or astrology, medicine, and philosophy,

which belong only to this world

cannot reach to the seventh sky (Divine knowledge).

-Rumi

Sohrab Sepehri invites us to camp beyond the fences of knowledge, as he very well knows that our knowledge cannot take us very far; the secret of the red roses cannot be revealed in such territories.

Discovering the secrets of the roses is beyond our attempt.

Maybe we are meant to float into the magical charm of the roses,

And perhaps, through lilies and centuries, to run after the song of the truth.

Let's camp beyond the borders of knowledge.

More knowledge means more questions, because science/knowledge is caused by questioning, and questioning arises from knowledge. Avicenna encountered a world of questions as the consequence of his vast amount of knowledge. Nevertheless, he understood the point of that experience, that he still did not know anything; in fact, he came to realize his ignorance:

My knowledge advanced high enough to understand that I am rather ignorant.

Or as *Abu Saeed Abil Kheir* says:

Although my heart much sought in this vast land [of creation],

it did not find a thread (it didn't get to know even the tiniest bit),

in spite of much details that it explored.

From my heart rose thousands of suns,

Still could not reach the mystery of the Kamal of a tiny particle.

Or:

The building and garden of the school,

noises and arguing of science,

We have abandoned them all, for the sake of the wine-jar and the gorgeous Saki, server of the wine.

-Hafez

Our notebook of knowledge, wash it all with wine,

Because I saw the heavens are distant from the heart of the wise.

-Hafez

Therefore, science, despite its tremendous illuminating conclusions, can never find the solution to the puzzle of creation, and as each day passes, the proportion of the things man does not know (to that of his knowledge) increases.

The Reasons for Disconnection from the Interuniversal Consciousness and the Protective Layer Cut off

It is expected that all the issues leading to a disconnection from the *Interuniversal Consciousness* to be taken into account with precise attention to prevent any likely future problem/s. It is necessary to remind you that in some circumstances according to the discretion of the Network, and despite the protective layer and the connection being in place, still there is a possibility of the spiritual awareness and revelation being cut off.

The reasons for disconnection from the *Interuniversal Consciousness* and cut of the Protective Layer are as following:

A. All actions and activities that prevent the ascendance and advancement of the collective soul of the society, and prevent others from being guided and led toward the Interuniversal Consciousness, such as:

•Evading and refusing to give information and awareness about the Network to those whom are interested and eager; depriving them from being easily connected to the network (as easily as the user himself is connected), and from using its blessings for reaching *Kamal*.

•Presenting false information and deceiving people by pretending that the individual is involved in a special connection via special [holy religious] figures, which has enabled them to access the network's facilities. This causes disappointment in others and prevents those who are eager from easily accessing this Divine mercy. It also prevents them from knowing that they can easily have access to the network, misleading them from the main path, and depriving them of the possible insight, wisdom, and true enlightenment which means clear-sightedness and spiritual insight and illumination, clarity of vision about existence, and understanding of the universe.

B.Uses against the interest and welfare of humanity, such as:

•Desire to use the network's capabilities in order to fulfill negative thoughts such as intruding [others privacy and sacred boundary] and gaining power over others, mind-reading, desire to access others private characteristics, and using it in a way that causes them material or spiritual loss and harm, jeopardizing their security. And all similar acts that are against divine justice.

•**Discrimination** in presenting the services of the Network to others.

C.Acting against the network's reverence such as:

•**Doubts, denial, ungratefulness, and so on, toward the network.**

•**Denial of what you have attained** through the network, which causes the magnificence and glory of *Interuniversal Consciousness* to remain hidden and uncovered from others, thus causing them to remain ignorant. Also, pretending that the performed activities have originated from elsewhere than the Circle (Halqeh) of Unity and the Network (Divine consciousness).

• Any abuse in the name of the Network

• Putting any name (even the names of holy figures and saints) in highest [place] instead of the name of God and His Consciousness.

"We ask help (for each and everything), only (and absolutely), from You "
-Quran; Faatihah: 5

Therefore, as soon as you realize that your protective layer has been cut off, in addition to refraining from working in this area, you must report this immediately to your master.

The Principle of Unity of the Path

Becoming familiar with the *Interuniversal Consciousness* and observing how it works in practice, and the miraculous transformations that happen as a result of linkage to this Network, and doing positive and humane activities in this respect, make us feel closer to such extraordinary and spectacular Divine phenomenon every day. It also leads us closer to the perception of the unity that governs the universe, the unity that joins all the constituents of the universe together and constantly calls out the message that "the universe is one unified body" into the ears of the vigilant and aware-hearted individuals:

All this reflection of wine and varied images that have appeared into the cup,

Is a splendor of the face of the wine server (Saki).

-Hafez

It is a message that takes us beyond the borders of human thoughts and contemplations, and places us at the uttermost peak of human intellect and worldview, and in addition to reaching the level of awareness of us being parts of one unified body; it enables us to understand that:

The heart and soul of the universe is all one body.

Not only a body, but indeed a jewel.

From this perspective, the extent of our field of view, thought and perception can expand not only beyond ethnic, tribal, national, racial, and even international boundaries, but the entire universe or at the "Interuniversal" level.

According to the Interuniversal *Erfan* without the perception of the universe and the consciousness ruling it, the human being will always live in multiplicity, confusion and perplexity, and all the roads before him will come to a dead end. This deep perception is the result of becoming familiar in practice with Divine consciousness, the consciousness governing the material world. This consciousness (which serves as the means) has guided us to the unity of the universe (that serves as the aim), via the unity of the path (that serves as the way).

The essential condition for reaching unity is that all the factors encompassing and defining this unity must be in unity themselves. Therefore, we can understand that *it is not possible to be in multiplicity of the paths and still reach unity.* This means that the individual cannot reach unity by mixing several different paths together, for the reason that the chosen different ways may oppose one another in the frameworks that they analyze and implement, although they may all serve a common purpose.

Come, Saki, come, as your act is removal of duality, fill me with unity, and remove my multiplicity.

-Molana Rumi

Although there are several different paths for reaching this unity, there may exist different ways as per number of the people in the world, yet each way, by itself, should be in total unity. Multiplicity in the path itself creates [further] multiplicity, and results in conflict and perplexity [for the followers]. For example, in some paths, the act of strict discipline and physical suffering, seclusion, withdrawing and isolation from the society is used, whereas in other doctrines this might be considered highly erroneous, as it surely is considered in Interuniversal Mysticism.

Universal unity is the same as Divine unity, and the day a human being comes to perceive this unity and sees himself in unity and coherence with the universe, it reaches the boundary of becoming God-like and seeing as God sees. That is when everywhere we turn; we can perceive the light of His face[10][manifestation] and see nothing except Him.

Human beings can attain such a state, that they see nothing except God.

Behold the true excellence of the status of being a human.

-Saadi

I turn into the direction of a red rose when I pray.

I stand in a spring while I perform my prayers.

I bow and put down my forehead on the light,

My prayer carpet is the grassland...

-Sohrab Sepehri

And whatever one sees before his eyes, is perceived as nothing but Divine manifestation, and one has been privileged to perceive this:

("Whithersoever you turn; there is the Presence of God"

- Quran; Baqarah: 115)

Following this, we understand the richness and deepness of Sepehri's insight:

My Kaaba is by the rivers,

My Kaaba is under the branches of Acacia;

My Kaaba is like the breeze, travels form one garden to another,

and it goes from town to town.

My Hajar-al-Asvad is the glow of the flower-bed.

Through the perception that the universe is one unified body, we can reach the status of "Having no Qibla."

Don't seek for one Qibla here, as there are six [or more] directions to this Motherland.

The real Qibla is having no home (the homeland is the whole universe),

---

10- Please note that 'face' has been used here metaphorically, and by no means does God possess any physical feature.

Let's build a nest in 'non-being'[11].

-Molana Rumi

And it is only then that whatever direction we look, we see His manifestation; indeed from observing the effect, we conclude the existence of the owner of the effect (the cause).

Look clearly, because the light which you call the "moonlight"

is indeed the "sunshine."

-Shah Nemat Allah Vali

By observing the moonlight [Effect], indeed, we have concluded the existence of the sun [Cause]. The sunshine that is from the very sun into which we dare not look directly for even one second, as our eyes cannot stand its light.

******

At the end, **we invite everybody again to comply with the principle of unity of the path: to avoid mixing and combining different ways and methods simultaneously without considering, studying, and researching their opposing aspects.** Thus, one can avoid confusing himself and others from future perplexities that have been observed in many occasions.

Let us not forget that the final destination and our purpose are to reach the Interuniversal unity through the practical acquaintance with the Divine consciousness. All the individual's activities in Interuniversal Mysticism must comply with this purpose, otherwise, these activities lack the necessary mystical (*Erfan*-based) and spiritual values, and would serve merely to increase the individual's egocentricity and act of showing off.

Definition of Interuniversal

Interuniversal, in summary, is an indication of the perspective of *Erfan-e* Halqeh about the universe, which includes the ascendance of the level of human thoughts up to the entire universe. Thus, we desire to think beyond and above

---

11- ADAM or Non-polar world: The world that is totally out of the scope of human perception and thus can not be described.

all the ancestral, tribal, racial, national, and other limitations, and to reach the perception of the universe through the perception of Divine communal mercy. We believe that without perceiving the "whole", one cannot draw an appropriate map or purpose for the path of *Kamal*.

A constituent, what does it know about the way to its whole?

Unless the whole sends a guide for him.

Thou the whole Eshq! Pull me forward as a piece of yours,

As here I am helpless in the midst of conflicts.

It's like I am carrying the load of the whole world, from [the pain

of your] separation.

It's like I am a pillar carrying the load of the universe.

-Molana Rumi

The human being has reached a point where he deeply needs the understanding and knowledge of the whole, and to reach this, he must free the boundaries of his limiting thoughts and release himself from becoming involved in the pointless or less valuable details, and become capable of perceiving the ultimate purpose with the help of the Halqehes of *Ettesal* of Divine communal mercy. This enables him to access the knowledge of *Kamal*, without which the human being can never understand the destination and purpose of his coming and going.

The windmill never gets to know the purpose of its turning round,

Which it is the basis of the baker's trade and our bread.

Water pushes it round, thus it moves around [without knowing why].

If God cuts the water, it will stand still.

-Molana Rumi

If man does not communicate with the whole, he becomes like the windmill that does not know for what purpose it turns, whereas the understanding of this purpose is one of the human being's important missions.

Centuries of experience in interacting with details and sinking into them have demonstrated that human beings have lost their golden opportunities and yet have not reached any safe clue or means; because this [detailed] information has not been interrelated and correlated with the knowledge of *Kamal* and the 'whole' wisdom; therefore, human beings have pointlessly spun around themselves.

There are many differences between the human being and a windmill. A windmill may not be able to communicate with its whole and may not understand the cause and purpose of his rotation; whereas, the human being is a creature that can communicate with the whole and can understand the role he is supposed to play in the universe.

The time has come for fundamental reconsideration in our viewpoints, and reevaluation of all the things that in practice have not brought us wisdom and awareness of the whole. Like an impartial observer, we must consider and analyze our faults justly [without prejudice] to reach the perception of *Kamal*.

From the Interuniversalistic point of view, concentration means becoming a prisoner of one spot, one word, one field, and so on, whereas Interuniversal perspective proposes the opposite of becoming a prisoner, and follows the freedom of mind and expanding the boundaries of mind's capabilities. This is because perceiving and understanding the consciousness that governs the world and the One in possession of it, requires a free and capable mind; a mind that does not assume God as only the God of skies but knows He belongs to every time and place. Perceiving God as being present everywhere is difficult for the ordinary mind; therefore, some people are searching for Him only in the skies when they need Him to do something for them.

When we seek God either inside or outside, sometimes hidden and sometimes apparent, we are ignorant of the principle that God cannot be divided into pieces and He must be seen as an [absolute] whole.

Give up search and you will find.

Suspend your mind and all will bind.

The deeper you dive the surface hides.

The surface you seek the depth confides.

The core and shell are all but one.

So rest your soles, for here you're found In His presence, safe and sound.

-Molana Rumi

The Interuniversalistic view, in *Erfan*-e Halqeh, studies God as He should be understood, and prepares the individual's mind for such recognition. In this perspective, God is present everywhere, and the universe is His presence. He is not only the God of the skies and contrary to what has been dictated into human beings' subconscious, He is closer to us than the veins of our necks and we can feel His presence even near us on Earth. God belongs to all and every place nevertheless the human being calls upon Him only where he is in need, and otherwise He is not sought. God belongs to all times, yet again human being wants him only for special occasions.

In summary, the human being has a very incomplete perception of God, and as a result he has been unable to find an appropriate answer regarding his relation to God.

God has only one definition that is common among all people, while the subject of all human beings' common basis of thought is recognition and ways of reaching out to God.

Any pathway that is explored if it leads to You is magnificent.

Reaching You in any direction that is sought is wonderful.

Any face through which they can see Your face, is lovely.

Calling Your name, in any language that is spoken, is beautiful.

-Abu Saeed Abil Kheir

Wishing you Divine Grace

Mohammad Ali Taheri

Printed in Great Britain
by Amazon